Nursing Standards
&
Nursing Process

Nursing Standards & Nursing Process

Edited by

Marion E. Nicholls, R.N., M.S.

Associate Professor of Nursing
Department of Nursing
Russell Sage College
Troy, New York

Virginia G. Wessells, R.N., M.S.N.

Nurse Coordinator
Cancer Rehabilitation Project
Medical College of Virginia Cancer Center
Virginia Commonwealth University
Richmond, Virginia

Contemporary Publishing, Inc.
Wakefield, Massachusetts

Library of Congress Catalog Card Number: 76-56882
International Standard Book Number: 0-913654-31-0

Type set by TKM Productions, Peabody, Massachusetts

Manufactured in the United States of America by the George Banta Company, Inc.

Grateful acknowledgment for permission to reprint is given to: The Journal of Nursing Administration, Inc., W.B. Saunders Company, and The American Journal of Nursing Company.

Contributing Authors

Georgia Autorino, R.N., M.S.

Instructor in Nursing
Russell Sage College, Troy, New York

Barbara Ann Beeker, R.N., M.Ed.

Associate Professor of Nursing
Co-Director, Curriculum Revision Project
Russell Sage College, Troy, New York

Doris Bloch, Dr. P.H.

Chief, Research Grants Section
Nursing Research Branch
Division of Nursing
Department of Health, Education, and Welfare
Bethesda, Maryland

Nancy Repass Bullock, R.N., M.P.H.

Assistant Chief of the Bureau of Public
Health Nursing and Clinical Services,
Richmond City Health Department
Richmond, Virginia

Alla T. Campbell, R.N., M.S.N.

Former Cardiology Clinical Specialist
University Hospital
Augusta, Georgia

Marjorie Moore Cantor, R.N., Ph.D.

Associate Director of Nursing
Staff and Program Development
The University of Iowa Hospitals and Clinics
Iowa City, Iowa

M. Elizabeth Carnegie, R.N., D.P.A.

Editor, *Nursing Research*
New York, New York

Kristine Gebbie, R.N., M.N.

Assistant Professor of Nursing
St. Louis University School of Nursing
and Allied Health Professions
St. Louis, Missouri

Leon S. Geoffrey

Executive Director
Virginia Professional Standards Review
   Foundation
Charlottesville, Virginia

Mary Beth Hanner, R.N., M.P.H.

Assistant Professor of Nursing
Russell Sage College, Troy, New York

Mary E. Hogan, R.N., M.A.

Assistant Professor of Nursing
Russell Sage College, Troy, New York

Linda Stevenson Kimball, R.N., M.S.

Assistant Professor of Nursing
Russell Sage College, Troy, New York

Ann F. Klein, R.P.T., B.S.

Staff Member, Rehabilitation Department
Richmond Nursing Home
Richmond, Virginia

Mary Ann Lavin, R.N., M.S.

Research Associate in Hypertension
Washington University School of Medicine
St. Louis, Missouri

Marion E. Nicholls, R.N., M.S., G.N.P.

Associate Professor of Nursing
Russell Sage College, Troy, New York

Pamela L. Schell, R.N., M.S.

Staff Nurse in Ambulatory Care
Veterans Administration Hospital
Durham, North Carolina

Barbara J. Stevens, R.N., Ph.D.

Assistant Professor of Nursing Service
    Administration
University of Illinois
College of Nursing
Chicago, Illinois

Virginia G. Wessells, R.N., M.S.N.

Nurse Coordinator
Cancer Rehabilitation Project
Medical College of Virginia Cancer Center
Virginia Commonwealth University
Richmond, Virginia

Marie J. Zimmer, R.N., M.S.N.

Director of Nursing Service
University Hospitals, Center for Health Sciences
Professor, School of Nursing
University of Wisconsin—Madison

Contents

PREFACE

This book is the outcome of a long-standing frustration suffered by its authors-editors. As teachers in a baccalaureate school of nursing in the late 1960s, we were charged with instruction in the management aspects of nursing to senior students, and we spent many hours searching for suitable resource material for our course. This required perusal of a vast amount of literature produced primarily by social scientists and management experts. Application of management concepts to nursing required definition of the management role of the nurse and description of her use of management process in nursing. An essential management function is setting standards; yet there is little to help the student learn to carry out this function in relation to direct nursing care.

We discovered that our students could rarely define the word *standard* or identify a safe minimal standard of care without direction. Moreover, they knew little about how standards are derived and the many factors that influence standard setting and maintenance. We were also concerned because the courses in clinical nursing encouraged the student to identify a maximum standard of nursing care for individual patients and to work one-to-one with a patient, using this standard. We realized that as nursing practitioners in direct contact with the patient, they must be able to differentiate between maximal standards of care and minimal safe standards in order to achieve legal standards of nursing practice. We believed that in the "real world" of practice the nurse would sometimes achieve a maximum standard of care, but more often would achieve something between minimum and maximum, and that her legal mandate is to achieve the minimal safe standard for both individual and groups of patients at all times. Moreover, the use of nonprofessional personnel requires that the nurse play the role of group leader. Nursing students had to learn to use unfamiliar control methods to obtain the necessary data to make decisions about the safety and effectiveness of the nursing care being given, both by herself and other personnel. "Management Shock" was not uncommon among our students, but the result of their efforts encouraged us to pursue development of material needed to help them acquire the basic knowledge needed for standard setting.

It is the aim of this book to assist the student or the beginning practitioner of nursing to understand (1) the language of standard setting, (2) selected frames of reference in which this terminology is used, (3) factors affecting standards, (4) nursing process, quality control, and their application in standard setting and maintenance at the direct care level of practice.

The anthology approach enabled the authors-editors to select pertinent material from existing articles as well as to use original articles. Since the subject matter, frames of reference, and terminology used in this book are in a state of flux, the nurse needs to remain flexible in her thinking and alert to changes and their implications. We believe that her role in setting and maintaining standards is a crucial one and will move her into the spotlight as peer review comes to the forefront, as health care clients make their wishes known, and as federally legislated regulations are enforced. We hope that this book will help nurses* perform standard setting tasks well.

The first unit of this book provides an introduction to the changing vocabulary of both nursing standards and quality assurance programs. Factors affecting the devel-

opment of standards at the practice level are identified and discussed in the second unit.

The third unit focuses on the actual process of standard setting in direct nursing care, and the final unit is devoted to a series of case studies, with discussions of standards and quality assurance programs written by a group of practicing nurses and teachers in a variety of nursing settings.

We wish to acknowledge the contributions of the many students who challenged our thinking and required us to become more explicit in our explanations of nursing standards and quality control.

Neil Wessells provided patience and support, as did William and Elizabeth Hufford. We gratefully acknowledge their assistance.

We wish to thank *The American Journal of Nursing*, W.B. Saunders, and Contemporary Publishing, as well as the authors of the eight articles, for their permission to reprint in this book.

Thanks are also due to Joyce Conners, Gloria Francis, and Barbara Munjes for critique of manuscripts, and to secretaries Jean Cooper and Nicky Gloras, who typed the manuscripts.

---

*Nurses are referred to as *her* in the text of original articles for convenience. There is no intent to ignore the male segment of professional nursing; however, they are a minority at present.

Nursing Standards
&
Nursing Process

UNIT I

TERMINOLOGY AND NURSING STANDARDS

Introduction

As nursing increases its research activities, expands its body of knowledge, formulates theories and tests them in practice, the meaning of commonly used terms change and new terms are added to the nursing vocabulary. This unit is aimed at interpreting terminology currently in use in the areas of nursing process, standard setting, and quality assurance. As a result of the passage of Public Law 92-603, which established Professional Standards Review Organizations, nursing has felt pressure to develop more precise standards for nursing care and devise effective means to measure the degree of achievement of the standards. In order to do this, the profession has placed all nursing care activities under scrutiny, for standards are intimately involved with nursing process. This close examination has led to redefinition of old terms and addition of new ones.

It is increasingly obvious that terms which describe the two major areas in nursing, nursing process and nursing practice, are open to different interpretations. The ANA's *Standards for Nursing Practice* describe a nursing process as a standard for practice. A number of other authorities also describe nursing processes, often using terminology similar to the ANA's but not always having the same meaning. Thus, when one speaks of nursing process or nursing practice, it is not always clear what is meant.

With the increasing popularity of the problem-oriented medical record, another set of terms has come into use. The problem-oriented record is designed to encourage the use of a problem solving process. As this process and recording system have been adopted, they have also been adapted—with the usual changes in terminology.

In the past several years, a number of states have changed their definition of nursing and have included the word *diagnosis*. While it is a term well-known in medicine, it is relatively new to nursing. It is to be expected that there will be an increase in the sophistication of nursing diagnoses. The diagnosis of nursing problems is an essential element in setting nursing standards.

The term *quality assurance* is used to describe a process in which standards are set and action is taken to ensure achievement of the standards. As a process, it is well-known in business and industry, but has only recently become a part of health care practice. The introduction of Professional Standards Review Organizations forced first the medical profession and, now and in the future, all health care providers into rapid development of quality assurance programs. Some form of quality assurance program will eventually become a legal requirement for participation in federally financed health care programs such as Medicare. In all health care agencies, quality assurance programs will be in effect, and nurses will be expected to participate. Nurses should not only expect to participate, they should insist on participation in order to ensure that they have a voice in setting the standards for nursing care. To do this, nurses will need to understand the quality assurance process and its terminology.

Bloch's thought-provoking article speaks to the inconsistency of the definitions currently in use in nursing process, in problem-oriented recording, and in the definitions of nursing in Nurse Practice Acts. Bloch proposes a revised model of nursing process and suggests a partial definition of nursing practice that would provide for consistency in terminology between nursing process and nursing practice definitions.

To set a valid standard for nursing care, the nurse must be able to make an accurate nursing diagnosis. This requires a commonly accepted classification of diagnoses. Gebbie and Lavin describe the process used in identifying and classifying nursing diagnoses. They include a partial list of such diagnoses and suggest ways in which nurses can participate in the classification process.

Schell and Campbell describe the problem-oriented medical record very clearly and concisely. The nurse needs to become familiar with the terminology used in the original record system, as proposed by Weed, in order to understand changes in definitions of terms initiated by agencies that adopt the system.

The article by Geoffrey is included to provide concise basic information about the Professional Standards Review Organization, its operations, its semantics, and its implications for nursing.

Nicholls surveys the language of quality assurance and arrives at some common definitions of terms.

Chapter 1

Some Crucial Terms in Nursing— What Do They Really Mean?

Doris Bloch

A few years ago, while working on a nursing project, I found it necessary to define for myself the nursing terms *need* and *problem*, and I became acutely aware of some confusion in their use. I did not write down my thoughts at the time, because I wondered whether I might be playing a game of definitional acrobatics which would be of no importance to anyone but myself. But recently I came face to face with a semantic jungle in the form of a definition of nursing practice incorporated into a proposed nurse practice act. The terms used—"assessment," "problem identification," "implementation," "evaluation," and "health needs"—had a familiar ring. It became apparent to me, however, that the aggregation of these familiar terms into a definition was all but meaningless.

Such lack of clarity in a legal document concerned me greatly, and this concern became the acute stimulus that caused me to write down some of my thoughts about oft-used, but poorly defined, terms in nurs-ing—terms that represent concepts which are at the very heart of nursing. This chapter is, therefore, addressed to the meaning of some of those terms, such as *data collection, assessment, diagnosis, need,* and *problem.*

THE NEED FOR CLARITY

There are several areas in which these terms are used, and that is why it is important to clarify their meaning and come to a common understanding of them.

First, the terms to be discussed are often used in or are allied to the nursing process, a construct of basic importance in nursing. (Without the referent nursing, it can be considered the helping process, probably applicable to all professions, such as medicine, law, and social work.) The nursing process embodies such activities as assessment, plan-ing, implementation or intervention, and evaluation or, as conceptualized by others, observation, inference, validation, assessment, action, and evaluation[1-3]. Further, the principles of the nursing process seem to have been incorporated into ANA's standards of nursing practice, in which the following terms are most relevant to this discus-

Reprinted with permission from *Nursing Outlook*, Volume 22, Number 11, November, 1974, pp. 689-694. © 1974, The American Journal of Nursing Company.

sion: collection of data, nursing diagnosis, goal setting, plan of nursing care, nursing action, reassessment, and revision of plan[4].

The second and possibly most crucial area in which these terms are used is in the definitions of *nursing practice* in new nurse practice acts. One type of definition, found in a number of states around the country, appears to be based upon the nursing process, as the following excerpts show:

"...The assessment, problem identification, implementation and evaluation of the health needs of individuals, families, or communities...."[5]

"...The nursing assessment, evaluation of the patient and the administration of care to the ill, injured or infirm...." [6]

"...observation, assessment, diagnosis, care or counsel,...of the ill, injured, or infirm...." [7]

All these definitions, it will be noted, use terms associated with the nursing process. Other states, such as Indiana and Pennsylvania, follow the New York model, and speak of "diagnosing and treating human responses...."

The third area of semantic confusion relates to the problem-oriented record, which has the potential of becoming a valuable tool in both nursing practice and research. It, too, deals with such terms as data base, problem list assessment and plan [8,9]. And last, but certainly not least, a clear definition of terms is essential to sound research in nursing practice—an area in which precise definition of terms is crucial.

There appears to be much overlap among some of the terms in the citations above, and this raises questions which I believe to be more than semantic. What is the difference between a nursing problem and a nursing need? Is assessment the same as diagnosis? Does assessment refer to both data collection and problem definition? Does evaluation refer to evaluation of needs or to evaluation of the effectiveness of the intervention?

Answers to questions such as these are essential, I believe, in order to bring clarity to the meaning of the steps in the nursing process, to improve the definitions of nursing practice, to use the problem-oriented record to its full potential, and to create clear operational definitions in research involving the concepts underlying the terms under consideration.

THE REFERENT "NURSING"

The terms *need, problem, assessment,* and the like can be used with different referents, such as "health need," "nursing need," "nursing assessment," "medical diagnosis," and "nursing problem." My preference is for "health" as a referent, because when we use these terms we do not generally mean that we are assessing the needs of nurses, but rather that we are concerned with the health needs of patients. The use of the terminology in a news item headed "ANA Outlines Nursing's Needs to Congress" illustrates how subtle linguistic differences can reflect major differences in meaning [10].

In reality, we are dealing with a situation in which an array of different health workers is concerned with an array of "health" problems of patients, families, or communities. Health problems are assessed and addressed by the various health workers (such as doctors, nurses, social workers, and physical therapists), all with a somewhat different emphasis, but with a rather high degree of overlap.

A "nursing problem," then, is a patient health problem which is expected to respond to the type of action or intervention carried out by a nurse, and a "medical problem" can be conceptualized as a patient health problem expected to respond to the type of action carried out by a physician. This interpretation seems to be congruent with a statement by Gebbie and Lavin who say, in reference to *nursing diagnosis*, "It is the identification of those patient problems or concerns most frequently identified by nurses... which are amenable to some intervention which is available in the present or potential scope of nursing practice" [11].

It seems to me that there is much more stability in the term *health problem* than in the term *nursing problem*, because health problems do not change with changes in the roles of health workers. Hypertension, for example, is and always will be a health problem, but whether it is a nursing or a medical problem depends on our definition of the roles of the nurse and the physician at any point in time. What is a medical problem today may be a nursing problem tomorrow, and a medical diagnosis of today may well be a nursing diagnosis tomorrow. Therefore, I do not consider terms such as "nursing" problem and "nursing" diagnosis ideal; they are, however, convenient phrases which need not be discarded, so long as their meaning is clearly understood by all who use them.

DOES "NEED" EQUAL "PROBLEM"?

As one scans the literature in nursing, it becomes evident that the terms *need* and *problem* are used quite imprecisely. In fact, they are very often used interchangeably, despite what I believe to be a fundamental difference between them.

Thus, in an early paper reporting on a study of "extra-hospital nursing needs," Mickey refers to 18 categories of *needs*, while in an article about the same study five years later, she refers to 18 categories of potential health *problems*. One aspect of the study was to evaluate the intensity of identified needs, and again one notes the interchangeable use of the terms: "...the interviewer makes judgments for each applicable category about the intensity of the need (or health problem)..." [12]; "intensity of need" is later defined as "a measure of the severity of the health problem" [13]. These illustrations are not meant to single out a particular author; it just happens that the nature of the study, namely its concern with "nursing needs," affords a particularly good illustration in the light of the present discussion.

The literature abounds with other illustrations. Schwartz, for instance, describes a study of the nursing and psychosocial needs of elderly ambulatory patients [14]. Two substudies were done, addressed to the "nursing" and "social" aspects of these needs, and this is reported as follows: "a study of nursing *needs* conducted by a public health nurse interviewer, and a study of the psychosocial *problems* of the same group of patients conducted independently by a social worker interviewer [italics mine]" [15]. Conceptually, the nursing and social variables referred to appear not to have been different, despite the different terminology; the effort appears to have been to assess nursing and psychosocial problems, as well as to determine patient needs.

Another illustration is provided in the report of a study entitled "Recognition of Family-Group Health Problems by Public Health Nurses." Although the authors largely refer to *health problems* in the paper, the interchangeable use of the terms *need* and *problem* is apparent in the following excerpt: "A health problem or need was classified...." [16].

Perhaps the most well-known reference to *nursing problems* is the listing of 21 items by Abdellah and others [17,18]. Examples of these items are "to maintain good hygiene and physical comfort," "to facilitate the maintenance of elimination," "to identify and accept positive and negative expressions, feelings, and reactions," and "to use community resources as an aid in resolving problems arising from illness.''

These examples make clear that the concept underlying Abdellah's use of the term *problem* differs fundamentally from the concept underlying the examples cited earlier. Most authors (including those who write about the problem-oriented record), when using the term *problem*, are referring to a patient's health problem, such as "anemia," "frequent illness," or "allergy to cats," implying a patient-centered orientation [19 –21]. Abdellah, however, apparently uses the term *nursing problems* to mean nursing functions or nursing goals, or, maybe *nursing's*—with the emphasis on the possessive—problems, with an apparently more nursing-centered orientation.

One wonders whether such subtleties of conceptualization might underlie, at least in part, the problems experienced in the use of an instrument, the *Nursing Problems Priority Inventory* (NPPI), based upon Abdellah's scheme and developed at the City of Hope in California. Perhaps the lack of clarity about what a nursing problem is contributed to the difficulties experienced in test development, affecting its reliability and validity [22].

SOME DISTINCTIONS

In my opinion, *need* and *problem* refer to two quite different concepts, despite the frequently interchanged use of the two terms in the nursing literature.

Webster defines *problem* as "a question, matter, situation, or person that is perplexing or difficult; a question proposed for solution or consideration." This points toward the operational definition of a *health problem* as "a deficit or potential deficit in the health status of an individual, family, or community that is believed to be in need of correction," or, as defined in a forthcoming

book on the problem-oriented record, a *problem* "...is anything which causes concern to the patient or to those providing his care" [23].

It may be instructive to examine a number of hypothetical examples of defined health problems, as presented in Figure 1, because it becomes apparent that the definition of a health problem will often require the definition of a constellation of problems, related to each other in what appears to be a cause and effect manner. Such in depth problem definition would seem to be essential in many, but not all, cases to point the way toward the appropriate solution to the problem. Clearly, the case of "too many children" because of non-use of contraception due to a lack of carfare points toward action in terms of referral to the Welfare Department (a "need" for money), while the problem of a husband's opposition must be addressed in a completely different manner, if indeed it is amenable to intervention at all.

Webster defines *need* as "a lack of something useful, required, or desired." I would suggest that *health need*, rather than being synonymous with *health problem*, actually refers to the action necessary to solve the problem; that is to say, a *problem* is solved by meeting a *need*. Referring again to Figure 1, the first hypertension patient "needs" education to increase his understanding, and that would presumably be the appropriate action for the problem as defined. What the third hypertension patient "needs" is a matter for conjecture, but it is clearly not education.

"ASSESSMENT" AND "DIAGNOSIS"

The meaning of neither *assessment* nor *diagnosis* is quite clear in the nursing literature. Freeman, for example, refers to *assessment* as "defining the nature and the essential particulars of the problem complex to be dealt

FIGURE 1. HYPOTHETICAL EXAMPLES OF HEALTH PROBLEM DEFINITIONS

Patient	Problem	Problem due to	Problem	Problem due to	Problem
1a.	Hypertension	Non-compliance with therapy	Lack of understanding of purpose and administration of medications		
1b.	Hypertension	Non-compliance with therapy	Lack of understanding		Mental retardation
1c.	Hypertension	Non-compliance with therapy	Wishes to die		
2a.	Too many children	Non-use of contraception	Lack of carfare to go to clinic		
2b.	Too many children	Non-use of contraception	Opposed to contraception for religious reasons		
3c.	Too many children	Non-use of contraception	Husband opposed to contraception		
3.	Measels, no complications				

with. . . ." [24]. She seems to see it as both fact-gathering and interpretation. Woody and Mallison, in a discussion of the problem-oriented record, seem to equate *assessment* with the *defined problem* (assessment: possible venous thrombosis) [25].

Bonkowsky, in a paper on the use of the problem-oriented record, seems to use the term *assessment* in two different ways. Under "Nursing Initial Assessment," for example, the listed items seem to fall largely under the rubric of *data collection* without a judgment factor, such as "baby sleeps in crib in same room with mother," and "baby takes 4 oz SMA formula q 3h." Under the same heading, however, is "appears normal on gross observation," which implies a judgment factor, and—under other "assessment" headings—are similar items that appear to be of a judgmental or diagnostic nature, such as "probably dermatitis due to Vaseline," and "development normal for age" [26].

The National Commission for the Study of Nursing and Nursing Education's model of nursing practice conceptualizes *assessment* to include "observation," "interpretation," and "evaluation" [27].

The quotations above point to the conclusion that the term *assessment*, as presently used in nursing, refers to both the process of data collection and the interpretation of such data. This conclusion does not seem to be completely congruent with the dictionary definition, since Webster defines *assess* as "to analyze critically and judge definitively the nature, significance, status, or merit of; determine the importance, size, or value of." In other words, while the dictionary definition of assessment implies a strong judgmental factor, it does not seem to include the aspect of pure, nonjudgmental data collection; the latter is, at most, implied.

The dictionary defines *diagnosis* as "the act or process of deciding the nature of a diseased condition by examination; a careful investigation of the facts to determine the nature of a thing; the decision or opinion resulting from such examination or investigation." Gebbie and Lavin see *diagnosis* as "the logical end product of...assessment," and they list as nursing diagnoses such items as "pain," "fear," "malnutrition," and "noncompliance" [28].

I would suggest that assessment in nursing be defined to include two separate processes: (1) *data collection* (the gathering of more or less objective facts without an interpretive component), and (2) *problem definition* (or the making of the diagnosis), where judgment is brought to bear on the data by critical analysis and interpretation. Problem definition or diagnosis does *not* refer to a plan of action or to the spelling out of needs (defined above as the solution to the problem). In this regard the following excerpt from the new definition of nursing practice in Indiana is of interest: "...deriving a nursing diagnosis which identifies the needs of the individual and/or family.... [29].

It seems unfortunate that the term *assessment* is not clearly and consistently defined and that it embodies two conceptually distinct processes; it is also unfortunate that the term *diagnosis*, although relatively clearly understood, has a strong medical connotation, because they are convenient terms to use. I would prefer them to *data collection* and *problem definition*—mainly, I think, because the latter two terms have a research, rather than a patient care, connotation. However, for the sake of clarity, as well as for the sake of "fit" with the problem-oriented record (which embodies a "data base" and "problem list"), it seems sound to proceed with the use of the terms *data collection* and *problem definition*.

REVISED MODEL OF THE NURSING PROCESS

In order for the foregoing discussion to help bring consistency and clarity to the use of concepts in nursing, a slightly revised model of the nursing process is suggested in Figure 2. It consists of five components which would appear to be compatible with the traditional concepts embodied in the nursing process, with the problem-oriented record, and with ANA's standards of nursing practice. The components are defined here as follows:

1. *Collection of Data*
   the gathering of information (objective and subjective) on the physical, social, and emotional aspects of the health status of individuals, families, or communities
2. *Definition of the Problem*
   the making of the decision(s) regarding the deficit(s) or potential deficit(s) in the health status of individuals, families, or communities that are believed to be in need of correction
3. *Planning of the Intervention*
   the making of the decision(s) regarding the action(s) believed to be appropriate to effect a solution of the defined problem(s)
4. *Implementation of the Intervention*
   carrying out the planned action(s)
5. *Evaluation of the Intervention*
   determining the degree of effectiveness of the action(s) taken in solving the defined problem(s)

The term *intervention* used in the model, as well as terms used by others such as *nursing care, nursing action, implementation, care,* or *counsel* could be thought of as skirting the conceptual reality that action taken to solve a health problem in nursing practice can indeed be considered treatment. To quote Webster again, to *treat* is "to subject to some process, usually for a definite purpose; specifically...to give medical or surgical care to." The use of the term *treatment* is new in nursing, just as *diagnosis* was a few short years ago, and it probably is still con-

FIGURE 2. A FIVE-STEP MODEL OF THE (NURSING) PROCESS.

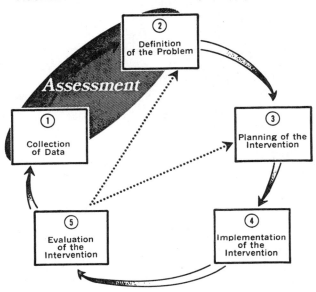

troversial. There is precedence for its use, however, since a number of the new nurse practice acts approach the definition of *nursing practice* in terms of "diagnosing and treating human responses to actual or potential health problems."

It would seem that the term *treatment* can conceptually encompass many types of action that nurses may take, including action of a care or cure nature, procedural or verbal action, and independent, dependent, or interdependent action. I chose the terms *problem definition* and *intervention* over *diagnosis* and *treatment* because of the strongly medical connotation of the latter two terms, and because the former are, in my view, perfectly good terms. However, the latter could well be substituted for the former in the proposed model without changing definition or meaning.

TERMS WITHIN A CONTEXT

Figure 3 is presented as a beginning attempt to place some currently used terms in nursing

practice into context, in the hope that it will help others to consider carefully their meanings and relationships.

The task that remains is to create a stronger and clearer definition of *nursing practice* out of the suggested model. This will probably take more heads than one, but I plan to suggest to the Maryland Nurses Association, Committee on Legislation, the following partial definition of *nursing practice*, which I believe to be identical in principle to the definition proposed in their draft document:

The practice of registered nursing means: the collection of data about the health status of individuals, families, or communities; the definition of nursing problems (where "nursing problem" refers to a health problem which is expected to be responsive to intervention by registered nurses); and the planning, implementation, and evaluation of intervention designed to solve the identified nursing problems. The purpose of such data collection, problem definition, and intervention is to maintain health, to prevent disease, and to promote recovery from illness or disability.

FIGURE 3. CONTEXTUAL SCHEME FOR SOME CURRENTLY USED TERMS IN THE CONCEPTUALIZATION OF NURSING PRACTICE.

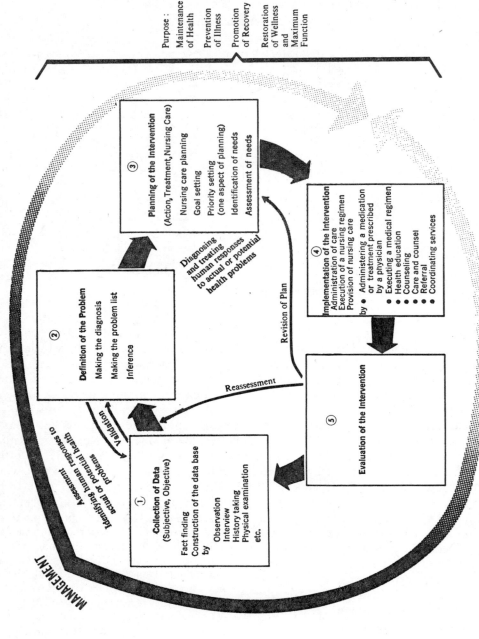

In the classic *Through the Looking Glass*, Humpty Dumpty said to Alice: "When *I* use a word, it means just what I choose it to mean—neither more or less." To which Alice replied: "The question is whether you *can* make words mean so many different things" [30]. We can, of course, go along with Humpty Dumpty and make words mean many different things, but I would suggest that we go with Alice and question crucial terminology.

REFERENCES

1. Michigan Nurses Association: Position on Nursing Practice. East Lansing: Michigan Nurses Association, 1971.
2. District of Columbia Nurses Association: Statement on Nursing Practice. Washington: District of Columbia Nurses Association, 1973.
3. Carrieri, V.K. and Sitzman, J. Components of the nursing process. *Nurs. Clin. North Am.*, Vol. 6, Mar. 1971, pp. 115–124.
4. American Nurses Association: Standards of Nursing Practice. Kansas City: American Nurses Association, 1973.
5. Maryland Nurses Association: Nursing Practice Act. Baltimore: Maryland Nurses Association, 1974.
6. Arizona State Board of Nursing: Law Regulating the Practice of Nursing in Arizona. Phoenix: Arizona State Board of Nursing, 1973.
7. Law Regulating the Practice of Registered Nursing. Washington (State): Senate Bill No. 2213, Chapter 133, Laws of 1973.
8. Woody, M. and Mallison, M. Problem-oriented system of patient-centered care. *Am. J. Nurs.*, Vol. 73, July 1973, pp. 1168–1175.
9. Schell, P.L. and Campbell, A.T. Problem-oriented medical records. POMR—not just another way to chart. *Nurs. Outlook*, Vol. 20, Aug. 1972, pp. 510–514.
10. ANA outlines nursing's needs to congress. *Am. J. Nurs.*, Vol. 73, July 1973, p. 1140.
11. Gebbie, K. and Lavin, M.A. Classifying nursing diagnoses. *Am. J. Nurs.*, Vol. 74, Feb. 1974, pp. 250–253.
12. Mickey, J.E. Studying extra-hospital nursing needs: a preliminary report. *Am. J. Public Health*, Vol. 48, July 1958, p. 883.
13. Mickey, J.E. Findings of study of extra-hospital nursing needs. *Am. J. Public Health*, Vol. 53, July 1963, p. 1048.
14. Schwartz, D.R., *et. al.*, *The Elderly Ambulatory Patient*. New York: Macmillan Co., 1964.
15. Schwartz, D.R. Nursing needs of chronically ill ambulatory patients. *Nurs. Res.*, Vol. 9, Fall 1960, pp. 185–188.
16. Lee, M.J. and Frazier, D.M. Recognition of family-group health problems by public health nurses. *Am. J. Public Health*, Vol. 53, June 1963, p. 935.
17. Abdellah, F.G., *et. al. Patient-Centered Approaches to Nursing.* New York: Macmillan Co., 1960, pp. 16–17.
18. Abdellah, F.G., *et. al. New Directions in Patient-Centered Nursing.* New York: Macmillan Co., 1973, pp. 529–530.
19. Woody, M. and Mallison, M. 1973, p. 1170.
20. Mickey, J.E. 1958.
21. Gane, D. Sparky: a success story. *Am. J. Nurs.*, Vol. 73, 1973, p. 1176.
22. Ayers, R. *et. al. The Clinical Nurse Specialist: An Experiment in Role Effectiveness and Role Development.* Duarte: City of Hope National Medical Center, 1972, pp. 21–22.
23. Wooley, F.R., *et. al. Improved Patient Care Through Problem-Oriented Nursing.* New York: Springer Publishing Co., 1974.
24. Freeman, R.B. *Community Health Nursing Practice.* Philadelphia: W.B. Saunders Co., 1970, pp. 57–58.
25. Woody, M. and Mallison, M. 1973, p. 1173.
26. Bonkowsky, M.L. Problem-oriented medical records: adapting the POMR to community child health care. *Nurs. Outlook*, Vol. 20, 1972, p. 517.
27. National Commission for the Study of Nursing Education: An Abstract for Action. Jerome P. Lysaught, (dir.), New York: McGraw-Hill Book Co., 1970, p. 65.
28. Gebbie, K. and Lavin, M.A. 1974, pp. 250–251.
29. Indiana State Nurses Association: Definition of Registered Nurse Practice in Indiana. Indianapolis: Indiana State Nurses Association, 1974.
30. Carroll, L. *Alice in Wonderland and Other Favorites.* New York: Washington Square Press, 1951, p. 190.

Chapter 2

Classifying Nursing Diagnoses

Kristine Gebbie
Mary Ann Lavin

Use of the term diagnosis is gaining acceptance as the logical end product of nursing assessment. Inclusion of the term in recently revised nurse practice acts and related bills reflects this acceptance not only by nurses but also by the public. And nursing diagnosis has been included in the generic Standards of Nursing Practice developed by the American Nurses' Association.

Perhaps we have hesitated to use "diagnosis" because so many of us automatically preface it with the adjective "medical" in our effort to be very clear that we practice nursing, not medicine.

While diagnosis may be a troublesome term to some of us, we must make it our own. And we must determine what legitimate nursing diagnoses are, their signs and symptoms or characteristics, and what interventions are specific to them.

While a standard classification system is no panacea for nursing's ills, it should, indeed, make many ordinary tasks much easier and aid us in focusing directly on those things which are essential to developing our contribution to overall health care. The level of our research can also be raised through the use of a standard nomenclature to communicate the content of our practice rather than the forms in which it is carried out.

DEVELOPING A SYSTEM

The first step in developing a classification is to identify all those things which nurses locate or diagnose in patients. This means nothing less than describing the entire domain of nursing. This does not mean the identification of all of the tasks performed by nurses or of all the things nurses have ever done in any situation or under any circumstances. It is the identification of those patient problems or concerns most frequently identified by nurses, problems which are usually identified by nurses before they are recognized by other health care workers, and problems which are amenable to some intervention which is available in the present or potential scope of nursing practice.

Reprinted with permission from *American Journal of Nursing*, Volume 74, Number 2, February, 1974, pp. 250–253. © 1974, The American Journal of Nursing Company.

The second step is to reach some agreement about consistent nomenclature which can be used to describe the domain of nursing as identified in step one. For nurses to collaborate effectively, even within one health care setting, much less across organizational and geographic boundaries, we must know what we are all saying. Terms should be sufficiently well-defined so that if a nurse from one setting says she cares mostly for patient with "x" nursing diagnosis, another nurse in another setting knows at once the problem she is referring to or can go to a recognized dictionary of nursing nomenclature for a concise description of the cardinal signs and symptoms. Hypothetically, this terminology or nomenclature can be expanded readily from diagnosis to intervention, for interventions should be diagnosis specific, rather than symptomatic. If we are communicating more directly about the diagnoses we treat, we should be able to be clearer about the treatments we actually apply or provide.

The third step in the classification process is the grouping of identified diagnoses (the labels) into classes and subclasses so that patterns and relationships among them can emerge. This process may involve the division of some labelled diagnoses into two or more distinct entities, and the merger of what first appeared to be different conditions under one label. In this process much of the work already done on philosophies and conceptual frameworks for nursing may be of help. Also, the study and labelling of the diagnoses may reveal some more appropriate classification system than those attempted by deductive processes.

The final step in the process is the substitution of numbers or equivalent abbreviations for terminology, so that data related to the various diagnoses can be manipulated more readily by machine or hand. Substitution of computer language for the usual diary-type of nursing notations does not as-sist in the manipulation of data—it merely compresses the amount of space needed to store data. If we can reach the stage where coding of the diagnostic entities and related interventions is possible, we will be able to use computerized data retrieval systems to gain access to multiple cases of a given problem or multiple instances in which a given intervention was used, and the process of nursing research should be speeded.

GROUND RULES

The First National Conference on Classification of Nursing Diagnoses, though only a beginning, was a significant beginning. Four "instant old proverbs" emerged from the planning process and served as a partial guide to participants.

1. We won't satisfy everyone, but we must be intelligible to many. There is no way that the beginning phase of a work project such as the classification of nursing diagnoses can make all practicing nurses perfectly happy. However, even the beginning work must be in a form and language which can be used by and be intelligible to the majority of nurses. Only then will it serve as a springboard for the continuing development of the nomenclature and classification.

2. If it comes to a pinch of time and energy in the initial stages of work, detail must be sacrificed for comprehensiveness. If the material developed is broad enough so that almost every practicing nurse can see that it has meaning for the diagnosis of problems she encounters in her daily practice, there will follow multiple opportunities to test the labels and develop the details. If only a small portion of the domain of nursing is covered in detail, and the rest ignored, few will be stimulated to continue the work.

3. We must not reject existing material for new merely for its newness, but we cannot wed ourselves too rigidly to the present merely to encourage rapid acceptance. There

is no point or merit in reinventing the wheel. If available materials or terms will serve our purpose, we should use them. It is always tempting to do something all over again just so the world will know it is really ours. However, if we really can't agree that the old terms serve our purpose, we should articulate new ones, because it is hazardous to attempt to bend an already existing concept. We may lose the meaning we wanted as we try to keep others comfortable with our language.

The more nurses who become familiar with the preliminary list of nursing diagnoses and begin testing them, the more opportunities we will have to quickly develop a sound, comprehensive system of classifying nursing diagnoses. The initial classification of medical diagnoses, which listed causes of death, was done over 300 years ago, and consisted of five categories which were neither comprehensive nor logically consistent with one another. It has taken the intervening 300 years to reach the sophisticated level of the International Classification of Disease and the Systematized Nomenclature of Pathology. The improved state of communication and our potential ability to learn from other disciplines should shorten our developmental time to considerably less than 300 years, but it will take many more years than three, or even 30.

The concepts developed must be tested formally. This can occur in research centers, in practice settings of all kinds, and in education settings. This involves the commitment, not only of the individual nurse, but of the nursing organization in the specific locale. Administrators, directors, and supervisors can be instrumental in the beginning of testing projects in their institutions.

PRELIMINARY DIAGNOSES

Because the conference participants could not agree on any one classification scheme for the diagnoses they identified, the diagnoses were listed alphabetically. Obviously, then, the order in which a diagnosis appears says nothing about its frequency of occurrence, importance for patient welfare, or relationship with those diagnoses which precede and follow it. The 30 diagnoses on which the group reached some consensus are listed in Figure 1.

FIGURE 1. TENTATIVE LIST OF NURSING DIAGNOSES.

Alterations in faith
Altered relationships with self
    and others
Altered self-concept
Anxiety
Body fluids, depletion of
Bowel function, irregular
Cognitive functioning, alteration in
    the level of
Comfort level, alterations in
Confusion (disorientation)
Deprivation
Digestion, impairment of
Family's adjustment to illness,
    impairment of
Family process, inadequate
Fear
Grieving
Lack of understanding
Level of consciousness, alterations in
Malnutrition
Manipulation
Mobility, impaired
Motor incoordination
Noncompliance
Pain
Regulatory function of the skin,
    impairment of
Respiration, impairment of
Respiratory distress
Self-care activities, altered ability
    to perform
Sensory disturbances
Skin integrity, impairment of
Sleep/rest pattern, ineffective
Susceptibility to hazards
Thought process, impaired
Urinary elimination, impairment of
Verbal communication, impairment of

Some of these labels may mean something to you, others may be so much Greek. Even if the clinical situation labeled by any of these diagnoses is identifiable, no diagnostic label makes real sense unless it is accompanied by a list of characteristics. By characteristics, we mean the signs or symptoms actually present in a person who has the diagnosis in question. This is not the same as assessment parameters, which serve as guidelines in selecting what to observe in order to determine whether or not the pertinent characteristics are present. If a characteristic of "urinary elimination, impairment of" is "output below 500 cc in 24 hours," the assessment parameter can be listed as "urinary output." The diagnostician must know the specific characteristics of a given diagnosis before making a judgment about the patient's condition.

For some of the identified diagnoses, no specific characteristics were listed. The participants could only agree that the problem was in the domain of nursing. To clarify this, we will compare the present levels of sophistication of the first three diagnoses: alterations in faith, altered self-concept, and anxiety.

Alterations in faith has three subdiagnoses: alterations in faith in one's self, alterations in faith in others, and alterations in faith in God. These can be further modified by two other concepts which were considered fairly significant in describing a diagnostic category: its etiology, whether anatomical, physiological, psychological, or environmental; and its duration, whether chronic, intermittent, acute, or potential. Some characteristics noted for this diagnosis were obstacles to responding in a love relationship to man and God, recognition of sinfulness, acceptance of one's self, and acceptance of others' needs for a relationship with God.

As you can see, these are not behavioral signs, nor are they necessarily symptoms which a person might describe himself as having. But even with this lack of clarity regarding the characteristics of this diagnosis, a sufficient proportion of those attending the conference believed that it was appropriate to be concerned about the patient's faith, at least in himself, and so the diagnostic label stands until further testing validates its inclusion and yields more specific diagnostic criteria, or leads to the exclusion of the category from the classification system.

Initial testing of this diagnosis would be anecdotal. Someone could collect records of any patients about whom a nurse says, "He's just lost faith," or "He seems to have given up." A list of the common characteristics from these records could be developed and this list of signs and symptoms could then become the basis of a wider case-finding effort. Or, perhaps, no commonalities would be found and we might learn that this diagnosis is meaningless and leads nowhere in the clinical situation.

Altered self-concept has four subdiagnoses: altered body image, depersonalization, identity conflict, and role disturbance. Again, each of these may have any of the four etiologies and any of the four durations. For example, an altered body image of anatomical etiology and chronic duration might be the diagnosis of a person who had lost a limb one year prior to contact with the diagnosing nurse and had not yet incorporated the loss into his image of himself. An altered body image of environmental etiology and acute duration might be the diagnosis of a patient forced to wear translucent goggles during a diagnostic procedure.

While no discrete characteristics were identified for all of these subcases, the subdiagnosis of altered body image is fairly well defined as being characterized by negative verbalization about the body, expressions of grief over the loss of a body part or function, nonverbal behavior (such as not looking at the body part, not touching the body part, hiding or overexposing the body part, purposeless activity, change in eye contact, change in hygiene), general reactions of poor comprehension of facts and explanations, changes in total self-concept (sexual roles, productive roles, and so on), and use of nonpersonal pronouns. Some of these characteristics also seem to apply to other subdiagnostic categories. We must, then, work to discover which are the general signs or symptoms which lead one to the general diagnosis of altered self-concept, and which are the finer distinguishing marks that enable one to apply one of the subdiagnostic labels. Work on clarifying this diagnosis could reach a more sophisticated level much more rapidly than work on that of alteration in faith.

The third diagnostic label is anxiety. Here, the conference participants drew on well-recognized portions of nursing literature and selected subdiagnoses in line with the four types of anxiety identified and studied by Hildegard Peplau [1]. These subcategories of anxiety are each described by discrete characteristics. If the patient's reason for concern or anxiety is not identifiable, the general diagnosis of anxiety is made and then a subcategory is selected, based on the following:

Mild anxiety: increased learning ability, alertness to environment, increased awareness of detail, increase in goal-directed behavior, restlessness.

Moderate anxiety: narrowing perceptual field, attention to detail, muscle tension, perspiration, needing help to focus problem solving.

Severe anxiety: very narrow perceptual focus or scattering of attention, inability to relate parts to whole, trembling, nausea, headache, feeling of dread, rapid pulse.

Panic: distortion of reality, extremely narrow focus, difficulty verbalizing feeling, bizarre behavior, dilated pupils, increased pulse, ashen color.

As with all diagnoses, these may be modified by their etiology. Anatomical etiology

did not seem probable, though some might want to research this. Examples of physiological, psychological, and environmental etiologies can be identified readily. The duration of an anxiety state can also be identified as chronic, intermittent, acute (situational), or potential. Research on this diagnosis might begin with the identification of all interventions ever used in conjunction with the diagnosis and move to the determination of which interventions yielded the most success in a given subdiagnostic situation.

Clearly, diagnostic development is an evolutionary process. An example of this can be drawn from the biography, *The Doctors Mayo* [2]. Having decided that *bellyache* was appropriate to the domain of medicine, someone began keeping records of all cases of bellyache. In reviewing these cases, someone observed the major distinction: some people had a fever and some did not. This process of making distinctions continued, coupled with distinctions in intervention. For example, surgery prior to or following the onset of abdominal rigidity led to the eventual identification of acute appendicitis as discrete from the generic acute peritonitis to which it sometimes leads.

The process of inclusion and exclusion of diagnostic terms involves decisions. At present there is no statement of the criteria for inclusion or exclusion though some might be inferred. Some labels were proposed which are not developed well enough for us to decide whether they should be included or eliminated. These diagnoses were depression, developmental lag, jaundice, sexuality problems, stress, and suicide-potential. Several other labels were discussed, accepted as preliminary, and then discarded. Dependent personality and drug dependence, for example, were identified and then discarded.

Dependent personality was eliminated because of the experiences other disciplines have had in attempting to label so-called personality types and the extreme difficulty of making the labels sensible and useful. Drug dependence was discarded because we had decided not to duplicate previous efforts, and the various types of chemical dependency are well categorized in the *Standard Diagnostic and Statistical Manual of Psychiatry*. There is no prohibition against using a label from another field if we use it with the characteristics and accuracy usually expected and it says what we want it to say.

We may well come to similar decisions regarding other diagnoses on the preliminary list. We may also subsequently decide to include labels which were eliminated or not considered during this first conference. That is for nurses to determine collectively.

FIRST STEPS

How can nurses everywhere take part in this? How does one begin? A simple method of primary data collection, which can be used almost immediately and can develop into sophisticated research designs, involves the cards used in medical records departments to cross-index medical diagnoses and procedures. When a patient is discharged from the facility, the face sheet of his record is numerically coded by the physician's discharge diagnoses and procedures. A card like this is prepared for each one of hundreds of medical diagnoses and procedures. The record number of each chart which was coded by that procedure or diagnosis is entered on the appropriate card. It is then possible to retrieve the last 100 cases of X or all examples of Y performed in an institution in 1971.

The card can be modified for nursing use. One nurse, a ward nursing staff, or the entire staff of an agency, could decide to keep records on one or more of the diagnoses on the preliminary list. Each time a nurse diagnosed a patient as having the problem in question, whether she used the characteristics listed in the preliminary manual or just said "I know that's what he has," she would enter the patient's name, age, record number, her own name, and other cross-referencing data, such as concurrent medical diagnoses or other nursing diagnoses also present, on the card for that diagnosis. Then, when sufficient cases are identified, the indicated records can be retrieved and studied to see if people were consistent in applying the label, if the chief criteria were readily identified, if our notes reflect what we say we saw, and how we intervened. If cards were kept for all the diagnoses and an attempt made to diagnose all patients, it would also be possible to review all the cards after a given time to determine the morbidity rate for each diagnosis so that attention could be focused on those which seemed to occur most often.

This approach is relatively simple and many people could be involved, even though only one or two people might do the final data analysis. Also, these cards are standard from institution to institution and duplicate copies of completed cards could be sent to a central data collection point. This would permit regional or national study of one or more diagnoses.

In their collective consciousness, nurses have a wealth of data about nursing. Together, we can develop a standard nomenclature of nursing diagnoses.

REFERENCES

1. Peplau, H. E. *Interpersonal Relations in Nursing.* New York: G. P. Putnam's Sons, 1952.
2. Clapesattle, H. *The Doctors Mayo.* 2d ed. Minneapolis: University of Minnesota Press, 1954.

Chapter 3

POMR — Not Just Another Way to Chart

Pamela L. Schell
Alla T. Campbell

The problem-oriented medical record (POMR) can revolutionize health care practice, the education of health practitioners, and the evaluation of health services. Properly used, this record system has tremendous implications for nursing as well as for medicine and other health care disciplines. Although one cannot be knowledgeable about all of the changes being proposed in the health care field, everyone working within it—particularly those who are shaping the future of health care in this country—should have some understanding of the concept of the problem-oriented medical record.

It was less than a year ago that we became aware of this system of medical record keeping developed by Dr. Lawrence Weed[1]. The system was being introduced into a nearby medical center, and Dr. Week was invited to describe his system to the staff. We attended his lecture and decided to examine this new concept more closely.

Since 1968, frequent references to the Weed system have appeared in medical journals, but only recently have two articles about it appeared in the nursing literature [2,3]. However, both those articles stressed only certain aspects of the system—improved charting, better communication among members of the patient care team, and improved patient care. While these are important goals of the POMR system, there is much more to this revolutionary health care concept.

PHILOSOPHY OF EDUCATION

In order to fully comprehend the implications of this system—particularly for the education of health care personnel—it is necessary to understand Dr. Weed's philosophy of education, which he described in the lecture that we attended:

> ...One of the premises [in education] has to do with memory...that there is a core of knowledge that people should know, that you should give it to them, that you should test them on it, that this will be useful in the

Reprinted with permission from *Nursing Outlook*, Volume 20, Number 8, August, 1972, pp. 510-514. © 1972, The American Journal of Nursing Company.

practice of medicine, [that] it's absolutely necessary, [that] you can then take their grades and equate them with how good they are [as practitioners] and with what they might do in the future. *My* premise is that there should not be a core of knowledge, that you should never have a memory-dependent system, and that you should teach a core of *behavior* so that the person becomes thorough, reliable, analytically sound, and efficient.

We have been conditioned to accept people who *know* a large number of facts as *educated* people, implying that memorizing facts is the process of education. The rapidly expanding scope and variety of facts that are part of medicine today, however, make a memory-independent system of education incongruous. Since our educational system perpetuates the illusion that our answers must come from memory if we are to function effectively, the time has come for educators in the health care disciplines to face up to reality. Total performance includes not only cognitive ability, of which memory is a small part; it also includes affective or attitudinal ability and manipulative or psychomotor ability[4]. Since a student can learn rather easily to extract facts from the literature, the educator's task should be to teach students how to deal with the facts in a thorough, reliable, analytically sound, and efficient manner[5].

The POMR is a means whereby this philosophy of education can lead to the achievement of specific, attainable goals. Through the development and proper management of the medical record, the performance of those providing patient care is exposed to critical assessment, just as scientific investigations are open to the evaluation of other scientists. An ongoing detailed scrutiny of records can also serve to promote professional growth and development. But, before discussing the many other implica-

tions that the POMR has for nursing, let us examine the system itself.

POMR COMPONENTS

What are the components of the POMR system? Basically, there are four main elements: a data base, a problem list, an assessment and plan for each problem, and progress notes for selected problems. (These and the following explanations and samples are based on Weed's problem-oriented medical record system.)

Data Base

The same type of baseline information obtained in the admission work-up—initial history, physical exam, and laboratory tests—and recorded in traditional medical records is included in the data base for the POMR. With the POMR, however, the information is standardized, which means that those concerned with the delivery of health care to a given population have defined the content of the data base prior to instituting the use of the POMR system. The specific information to be included is that which these practitioners believe to be necessary if they are to provide efficient, economical, comprehensive health care to the given population.

To assure uniformity and standardization of the data base, this information must be obtained from every patient who receives service. Properly developed, the system defines clearly what data must be collected in a consistent manner for each patient. The following example of a data base was developed for a population of cardiovascular patients in a medical center and, with use, it has been revised. Refining and updating the content of the data base increase its appropriateness to the population and are continuous responsibilities of those providing health care.

Chief complaint. A brief statement (if possible, in patient's own words) concerning his reasons for coming to clinic or hospital.

Patient profile. A brief narrative about the patient and his way of life that includes name, age, sex, race, occupation, hometown or area, referring physician, domestic matters (ages, number, and health of dependents; marital history; source and extent of income; living conditions), level of education and ability to read or write, religion, and how he spends an average day.

Psychological state. General statement regarding patient's present adjustment, including significant related factors.

Past history. Includes hospitalizations and dates, operations and dates, past illnesses and/or serious injuries and dates, medications for past conditions, smoking, drinking, and allergies.

Family history. Ages and causes of death of parents, grandparents, siblings, and children; history of congenital heart disease, diabetes, tuberculosis, rheumatic fever, high blood pressure, heart attacks, strokes, renal disease, cancer, mental illness; and age and health of living family members not previously mentioned.

Present illness. Brief narrative regarding present health problems, each discussed individually. Includes onset of the problem, progression, signs and symptoms, treatment (any attempts by patient to solve problem), and patient's understanding of the problem and its treatment.

Current medications. Those prescribed and taken as directed, prescribed and not taken as directed (explanation), self-administered, patient's knowledge of drug actions (if not recorded previously), administration and dosage, side effects, ability to obtain drugs, and any other significant factors affecting current medication regimen.

Diet history. Typical food consumption in a 24-hour period, whether a prescribed diet and its type, and patient's understanding of diet and any problems with it.

Present activity level and limitations. Stable, improved, or decreased tolerance in relation to last clinic visit, brief statement regarding how patient sees his present activity level in relation to past pattern of activity (active vs. sedentary life), and future activity goals (leisure time, occupation, etc.).

Present physical state. If patient has experienced any of the following or if any are noted by examiner, describe: angina (kind, pattern, changes), dyspnea, paroxysmal nocturnal dyspnea, orthopnea, cough; palpitations and/or tachycardia; dizziness and/or headache; visual disturbances; problems with hearing or speech; problems with orientation; syncope or blackout spells; numbness, tingling, claudication; nervousness, sweating, dry skin; pallor or cyanosis; fatigue or weakness; signs or symptoms of bleeding (nosebleed, hemoptysis, etc.); abdominal pain, nausea, vomiting; nocturia; edema; fever; pain other than previously mentioned; miscellaneous.

Physical exam. Skin (hair, nails, skin, turgor, color, temperature, etc.); neck (veins, carotids); lungs (rales, respirations, etc.); heart (rate, rhythm, gallops, murmurs); abdomen (liver); extremities (edema, peripheral pulses, color, temperature); neurological evaluation; BP/TPR, height, weight; obvious physical defects not previously noted.

Laboratory data. Blood work, urine, x-ray, electrocardiogram, etc.

PROBLEM LIST

Patient problems are identified from the data base. The more adequate and appropriate the data base, the more comprehensive the identification of problems. Problems are numbered, titled, and listed on a sheet at the front of the chart. This problem list is similar to a "table of contents" for the entire record. *All* the patient's known problems are listed—physiological, psychological, and socioeconomic.

A problem title is not entered as a specific diagnosis unless it can be unquestionably confirmed by the data. Therefore, each problem is titled according to the level of sophistication that is appropriate for it. Titles are changed as more information becomes available; for example, "jaundice," "blurred vision," and "poor memory" are acceptable problem titles. "Jaundice" may later become "serum hepatitis" or "carcinoma of the pancreas," when data confirm these diagnoses. Expressions such as "rule out," "probable," and "impression" are either diagnostic hunches or plans and should not be included in the problem list.

The problem list is updated by any member of the patient care team as more information is obtained, new problems are identified, or active problems become inactive. The team member (patient, physician, nurse, dietitian, and so forth) should communicate new information and make appropriate changes on the problem list or see that they are made. Maintaining a comprehensive, accurate problem list is a continuing responsibility of the patient care team, and the patient must be allowed to share in this responsibility. Many health practitioners review the problem list with the patient. It is the patient's record, and a complete problem list is an integral part of his care.

PROBLEM ASSESSMENT AND PLAN FORMULATION

Each problem is individually described and evaluated, and an initial plan is formulated for each one. These and all subsequent data (orders, plans, progress notes, etc.) are recorded in the body of the record under the numbered and titled problem to which they are specifically related. The majority of these entries follow a specific format (SOAP is the acronym) as indicated below:

Subjective data (S)—the problem from the patient's point of view, how he feels, any changes he has noticed.

Objective Data (O)—physical and laboratory findings, other pertinent observations or developments regarding the problem.

Assessment (A)—has the status of the problem changed? By what criteria?

Plan (P)—diagnostic plan, therapeutic plan, and plan for patient education.

Recording data in this manner encourages the development and use of sound logic in problem analysis and plan formulation.

PROGRESS NOTES AND RELATED DATA

Notations made by members of the health team other than the primary physician are not recorded as separate parts of the record; nurses notes, physical therapy notes, consultation or other notations are recorded as progress notes and entered in a continuing sequence. The series of progress notes regarding specific patient problems and the format (SOAP) requiring explicit recording of data are two means by which the POMR becomes a tool for improving communication among members of the patient care team.

For complex problems, flow sheets may be kept in addition to progress notes. The flow sheet is used to record specific parameters in a tabular or graphic manner. An example was devised for a clinic patient with multiple problems, including aortic stenosis, hypertension, obesity, nervousness and anxiety, and impotence (Figure 1). Monitoring various parameters is necessary for the proper management of complex problems. The patient care team devises a flow sheet to facilitate comprehending and interpreting

FIGURE 1. FLOW SHEET

Date		6-18-71	9-17-71	12/17/71
T-P-R		99²-70-16	98⁴-66-16	98²-64-18
B/P	Standing	160/90	162/88	188/128
	Lying	168/90	170/90	170/120
Headache &/or Blurred Vision		"Sev. Times a Week"	"Several times a week"	"2-3 x/week"
Edema		None	None	None
Anxiety		Mod-Severe	Moderate	Moderate
Sexual Function		Impotence x 2-3 wks	Continued Impotence	"Normal-Satisfactory"
Daily Activity Pattern		Stable	Stable	Stable
Weight		201 ½	204	196 ½
Electrocardiogram		Unchanged-Stable	Stable	Stable
Lab Data		WNL Except ↓ K⁺ (3.2)	WNL	WNL
Diet Since Last Clinic Visit		Low NA 1800 Cal.	Low Na 1800 Cal — ↑ Banana c̄ OJ intake	Low NA 1800 CAL
Medications Since Last Clinic Visit		Digoxin 0.25mg QD Diuril 500 mg qam Aldomet 250mg Tid	Digoxin 0.25 mg. q.d. Diuril 500 mg. q am. Hydralazine 10 mg q.i.d. Librium 10 mg. tid	Digoxin 0.25 mg QD Diuril 500 mg QA Librium 10 mg TID *Prescribed but not taken by PT: Aldomet 250 mg TID

changing, interrelated variables. The sheet helps the team follow the progress of such problems and may be the only progress notes in the record for certain rapidly moving problems.

ADVANTAGES OF THE SYSTEM

Properly developed, the POMR provides a logical, explicit description of all the patient's problems, the current treatment for each problem, and the plans of the health care team in relation to each problem.

Reviewing such a record is an efficient means of evaluating the team's performance and providing the team with immediate, meaningful feedback on the quality of patient care. Such a record audit thus becomes both an educational experience for health care personnel and an essential instrument for quality control of health care services.

However, a record system that may expose practitioners to criticism presents some elements of threat. Bjorn and Cross, who have used the POMR in their private practice for some time, report:

Most of us are not conditioned to welcome criticism, and we tend therefore to equate being corrected with being accused of stupidity or inferiority. Medical audits of the type described here, based on structured records, must become an integral part of medical practice if standards of quality are to be assured...Although we agree that it is more ego-threatening to be audited for performance than for knowledge, periodic audits of our practice have been exciting and intellectually rewarding exercises[6].

With the POMR, every time someone is audited, someone is educated; and every time someone becomes educated, someone receives better care—what Dr. Weed calls "the multiplier effect." Education of health care personnel and quality control of health services are concomitant and result in improved patient care. Because of the system's potential for change and improvement in health care, POMR has implications for current issues that nursing faces.

IMPACT ON NURSING EDUCATION

The report of the National Commission for the Study of Nursing and Nursing Education (NCSNNE) pointed to the need for developing a health core curriculum, which the commissioners defined as "a central body of basic knowledge, understanding, and skill that should be commonly known to all recognized health practitioners"[7]. This definition suggests what might be called "the old premise" in education. Using Dr. Weed's theory that a core of behavior rather than a core of knowledge should be taught, the definition might be: *a central body of behavior—all recognized health practitioners should be thorough, reliable, analytically sound, and efficient. The primary and common goal of all educational programs should be the development of our most basic resource—the individual's capacity to learn and think on his own.* Within this new frame of reference, the content and development of a health core curriculum would be viewed in a very different light.

Education is relevant when it teaches students a core of behavior which is applicable for a lifetime, rather than a set of facts that become outdated a few years after graduation. If we teach a core of behavior and use the POMR as a tool for monitoring that behavior, the student learns from real data. With this philosophy, there would then be no question about the relevancy of "training" in education programs[8]. However, there is question about any educational program that spends (wastes?) a great deal of time emphasizing the learning of facts.

The kind of learning that the POMR approach provides is applicable not only to basic nursing education, but also to continuing education. In fact, it is the essence of continuous learning. Nurses have seldom consistently had the challenge that the POMR can provide in their work-a-day world. Through daily practice in its use, nurses could experience the intellectual stimulation derived from sharpening their ability to define and assess patient problems explicitly and to plan, implement, and evaluate their patient care—not in isolation—but in coordination with the efforts of the interdisciplinary team. In addition, use of this new educational philosophy and concept of record keeping would alter the goals, content, and development of continuing education programs in nursing.

OTHER NURSING IMPLICATIONS

Other areas of nursing concern would benefit from use of the POMR. Chief among these would be research. The need for increased research in both the practice of nursing and the education of nurses has been recognized as one of the basic priorities for optimum change. The NCSNNE report contained many recommendations as to the kinds of research to be undertaken. However, good records are a prerequisite to scientific research and to clinical investigation for improving nursing practice and measuring the benefits of this practice for the client. Because the POMR, unlike traditional medical records, presents a logical and more explicit set of data, its use would make possible more *accurate* clinical research. Nursing then would be able to answer with greater authority the question: how can nurses be utilized more effectively, efficiently, and economically?

Another important question in nursing today involves licensure and related issues such as accountability, peer review, professional certification, and continued competency. Nurses are beginning to face the problem that a one-time licensing examination does not assure competency to practice for a lifetime. The POMR provides a tool for ongoing, meaningful audit, enabling nursing practice to be evaluated on the basis of readily available and definite criteria. Thus, the record would assist in the determination of professional accountability and continued competency in performance.

The evolution of professional roles in nursing, medicine, and other health professions has been recently receiving much attention. The expanding role of the nurse in areas long assumed to be the sole domain of the physician has prompted extensive discussion about the critical need for joint action among the professions in planning and articulating congruent roles. Expanded roles for nurses will require major adjustments in the orientation and practice of both nursing and medicine[9]. The problem-oriented system of record keeping and patient management could provide that common approach for nursing and medicine, as well as for other health professions. This mutual orientation would enhance collaborative efforts to define and develop congruent roles.

In addition, utilization of the POMR, with its improved documentation of clinical information and activities, would increase the accuracy of the cost-benefit analyses and similar economic studies recommended in relation to extended nursing practice[10].

CONCLUSIONS

The systematic method of recording utilized in problem-oriented record keeping illustrates the manner in which the system preserves recorded data in a standardized, explicit form. Familiarity with and use of this system are important to all members of the health care team and have implications for better, more comprehensive health care, as well as for improved methods of educating health care practitioners and evaluating the quality of patient care.

REFERENCES

1. Weld, L.L. *Medical Records, Medical Education, and Patient Care.* Cleveland: Press of Case Western Reserve University, 1970.
2. Bloom, J.T., *et. al.* Problem-oriented charting. *Am. J. Nurs.,* Vol. 71, Nov. 1971, pp. 2144–2148.
3. Field, F.W. Communication between community nurse and physician. *Nurs. Outlook,* Vol. 19, Nov. 1971, pp. 722–725.
4. McDonald, F.J. *Educational Psychology.* 2d ed. Belmont: Wadsworth Publishing Co., 1965, p. 391.
5. Weed, L.L. Medical records that guide and teach. Parts 1 and 2. *N. Eng. J. Med.,* Vol. 278, Mar. 14, 21, 1968, pp. 593–600; pp. 652–657.
6. Bjorn, J.C. and Cross, H.D. *Problem-Oriented Private Practice of Medicine: System for Comprehensive Health Care.* Chicago: Modern Hospital Press, McGraw-Hill Publications Co., 1970, p. 67.
7. National Commission for the Study of Nursing and Nursing Education. Summary report and recommendations.

8.   National Commission for the Study of Nursing and Nursing Education. p. 282.

9.   Extending the scope of nursing practice. *Nurs. Outlook*, Vol. 20, Jan. 1972, p. 48.

10. Extending the scope of nursing practice. p. 48.

Chapter 4

Professional Standards Review Organizations (PSROs):

What Are They and How May They Affect Nursing and Other Health Care Professions

Leon S. Geoffrey

Both those who favor PSRO and those who don't, agree on one thing— namely, that the real control of the PSRO program is at present vested in the Secretary of the U.S. Department of Health, Education, and Welfare (HEW). Any authoritative definition of the program or its elements must be sought from the officials of the department, or cleared by them if originating from another source. With that precaution in mind, we can proceed to describe the program from the perspective of a nongovernment organization attempting to assist the government in introducing it.

It is likely that the acronym PSRO is still something of a mystery to at least some readers. PSRO stands for Professional Standards Review Organization, as established by Section 249F of Public Law 92-603, which amended Title XI of the Social Security Act.

In a nutshell, PSRO can be described as the legally required review of all medical care financed under the Social Security Act for inpatients at hospitals and nursing homes. This includes Medicare, Medicaid, and the Maternal and Child Health programs. There is an optional feature in the law that could extend PSRO to ambulatory care at physicians' offices. This is not likely to take place nationwide in the immediate future, but it is being carried out experimentally in several states.

In October, 1972, when PSRO became law, its 17 pages of fine print were practically buried amidst numerous other highly technical amendments to the Social Security Act. These had been studied in detail by relatively few persons, and even members of Congress had only a limited notion of its contents. And yet, PSRO is now described by some as having a greater impact on medicine that any previous legislation. The PSRO legislation has been the center of a noisy and continuous controversy, but nonetheless has made considerable progress toward implementation. Whether the favorable results sought will be achieved depends on many factors. Only time and careful evaluation will provide answers on this subject.

What, then, are the issues and why all the fuss? Let's first examine the various elements of PSRO, then consider some of the arguments for and against it, and finally, bring our discussion down to how PSRO will affect nursing responsibilities in the hospitals and nursing homes.

Readers who will actually be involved in PSRO will need more thorough coverage of the subject than this brief paper can provide and may want to attend seminars sponsored by the PSRO in their area.

How is the PSRO function to be carried out, and by whom? For PSRO purposes, HEW divided the United States into 203 areas. A PSRO area consists either of an entire state, or, in the more heavily populated states, a group of counties. The physicians practicing in a PSRO area are invited (but not required) to set up a PSRO, and the expenses of this organization will be paid for under a contractual arrangement with the federal government. In addition to the area PSROs, there is a superstructure of councils at the state and national level, with ultimate authority for PSRO regulations being vested in the Secretary of HEW. Participants in PSRO do not hold the status of federal employees, but will be paid for their PSRO review activities from federal funds and will be operating in an environment of government regulation. It remains to be seen how these relationships will develop.

In areas where physicians fail to organize a PSRO, the Secretary of HEW may, after 1977, make other arrangements for conducting the function. He may appoint an organization such as a state health department, an insurance company, or possibly agents of the federal government to make the day-by-day decisions on case review. In other words, the law requires that PSRO be implemented. For example, the Medical Society of the State of Nevada went on record opposing PSRO, but the Secretary of HEW designated a PSRO there anyway.

After an area PSRO is formed, what will it do? Under the law, the PSRO will be responsible for determining whether admission of the patient to an institution (hospital or nursing home) is medically necessary; whether the length of stay in the institution is consistent with reasonable professional judgment; whether the services could be provided effectively and more economically by ambulatory care or by inpatient care in a different type of facility; and whether the quality of the services to the patient conform to appropriate professional standards.

To carry out its responsibilities, the PSRO will first develop and put in writing a series of documents known as *criteria*. These criteria will set forth what the area PSRO considers to be proper care, diagnosis, and treatment for each of the various patient health conditions, such as gastric ulcer, hip fracture, and so forth. Obviously, without such criteria there could be endless controversy as to the merits of any regimen of patient care in any case challenged by the PSRO review. There are two kinds of criteria documents—those to guide physicians, and those to be used by nonphysician health care personnel in reviewing cases to determine whether to accept them or to refer them to a physician adviser for further review and possible action. The latter are known as *screening criteria* and are the ones that nurses and other nonphysician personnel will use.

Second, the PSRO will use a system of panels of physicians to review cases, or a sample of cases, for reasonable conformity with the criteria. The PSRO may conduct this review directly, or, under certain conditions, may utilize the services of a hospital review committee and accept the findings of that committee as its own. Third, the PSRO will maintain what are referred to in the law as *profiles* on patients and on individual providers of health care. These profiles will provide a basis for PSRO decisions.

All of this does not mean that attending physicians will be required to treat their patients in accordance with the PSRO criteria. It does mean that they will have to explain to the satisfaction of the PSRO any repeated significant departures from the criteria. If any physician cannot or will not do this, then payment for his services will not be approved. In extreme cases, he may be barred from receiving federal funds for services to Medicare or Medicaid patients at any time. PSRO cannot tell him what to do, as its authority is limited to only one question—to pay or not to pay. However, it is easy to see why many physicians feel that, in reality, this payment authority will set new controls on the manner in which they practice medicine. Few want to spend much of their time giving explanations; it may be easier to go along with the criteria, whether they fit the particular patient situation or not.

The pros and cons of PSRO have been hotly debated, and physicians have been divided on whether to take part in it peacefully or to fight it. Those opposed to PSRO fear government regulation of the practice of medicine. Congress has determined the need for this control over the federal government's enormous expenditure of funds for health care, and HEW is charged with implementing the program. Cost containment, as well as improvement in the quality of health care, are major expected outcomes.

Perhaps the most cogent argument against PSRO is the possibility that although initiated with the intention of improving the quality of care, it may degenerate into nothing more than a cost-control mechanism. Previous experience with various federal health care regulations and their relative inflexibility has generated fear of bureaucratic domination, red tape, and unwarranted "lay" interference in what are considered strictly medical matters.

Physicians who favor PSRO believe that the peer review mechanisms incorporated in the law are long overdue. They believe that it offers a remarkable opportunity to bring about real advances in the quality of care. By spotlighting variations in present methods of diagnosis and treatment, new thinking will be stimulated; a process of continuing education of physicians and other health care providers will be operating, and this, they feel, will raise quality standards significantly.

A middle and more pragmatic view is that, since PSRO is now the law, it would be best for physicians to accept it and, through their own organizations, run it as effectively as possible rather than let others less qualified take over the job. At the same time, they can seek amendments to this law.

Under these circumstances, what can or should be happening at the individual hospital or nursing home?

First, the only safe assumption is that PSRO will remain for a long time. PSRO legislation may be amended, but it seems very unlikely that PSRO will go away. Should any form of national health insurance be legislated, it is sure to cause pressure for even more PSRO-type activity.

Second, each institution should continue to develop its capabilities to perform utilization review and medical care evaluation studies. Medical care evaluation studies, although emphasizing physician-ordered procedures at first, will undoubtedly be extended to all aspects of health care services. Not only will the performance of physicians be reviewed, but also that of nonphysician providers. Nursing performance will come under particular scrutiny, and in anticipation of this the American Nurses' Association (ANA) has been developing criteria of nursing performance that eventually will be built into the review system. In general, hospital utilization review committees were considered to have been relatively ineffective. That is one reason why PRSO is with us today. At present hospitals all over the country are engaged in a strenuous effort to upgrade their review committee capabilities, partly because they believe it is worthwhile, partly because the Joint Commission on Accreditation of Hospitals is mounting great pressure and providing new guidance, and partly because the hospitals hope to maintain their freedom when the PSRO sheriff arrives on the scene. This last motive may be justified, because there is a sub-section in the PSRO law that reads as follows[1]:

> Sec. 1155 (e)(1). Each Professional Standards Review Organization shall utilize the services of, and accept the findings of, the review committees of a hospital or other operating health care facility or organization located in the area served by such organization, but only when and only to the extent and only for such time that such committees in such hospital or other operating health care facility or organization have demonstrated to the satisfaction of such organization their capacity effectively and in timely fashion to review activities in such hospital or other operating health care facility or organization (including the medical necessity of admissions, types and extent of services ordered, and lengths of stay) so as to aid in accomplishing the purposes and responsibilities described in subsection (a)(1).

It cannot be assumed that good internal review will fully exempt an institution from PSRO surveillance. No group of physicians that has assumed PSRO responsibility can turn it over entirely to others. Few PSRO organizations would wish to serve as a rubber stamp. The most delicate relationship in the entire PSRO program is between the institution and the PSRO. The law recognizes this, and provides that the Secretary shall issue specific regulations on this point. In the absence of such regulations, a written agreement known as a *Memorandum of Understanding* can spell out the details and thereby prevent misunderstandings between the PSRO and the institution.

Third, all leaders in the health care occupations need to learn as much as they can as fast as they can about PSRO. By watching what happens in PSROs already established, they will be better able to adapt to the PSRO in their area when it assumes review responsibilities.

Fourth, nonphysician providers (including nurses) should accept any opportunity that arises to take an active role in PSRO affairs, particularly those that may involve planning or action outside their own institution. This is a very new program and each provider can influence it if he/she participates in it. Physicians have been given the primary role, but once they accept PSRO responsibility they will want to work closely with other health care personnel to build a successful system.

Fifth, all health care providers should make a great effort to improve records, since recording is a basic requirement for evaluation studies (which are essentially retrospective review).

PSRO is a complex subject. There are many questions yet to be answered and many changes yet to be made. The preceding essay gives the reader only a brief overview. PSROs usually begin as "Planning" PSROs, and are subsequently designated "Conditional" PSROs. It is when they reach the latter stage that they are given actual review authority under the law. Therefore, it is a good idea to determine the status of PSRO development in one's geographic area, to find out who is in charge and what is the *local* timetable for action.

Nurses, as the most numerous of the nonphysician health care providers, have an important role to play in decisions about quality health care, and their involvement in PSRO will increase.

REFERENCE

1. Section 249F of Public Law 92–603 of October, 1972. This amended Title XI of the Social Security Act by adding Sections 1151 through 1170. This quote is from Section 1155.

Chapter 5

Terminology in Quality Assurance

Marion E. Nicholls

Quality assurance, if not an understood or popular term, is probably the most frequently occurring one in nursing meetings and publications at this time. Federal legislation requiring that health care providers develop Professional Standards Review Organizations (PSROs) in order to be eligible to participate in federally financed health care programs has plunged nursing into a major effort to develop quality assurance programs. The effort is directed toward identifying quality nursing care, setting standards that reflect both quality and reality, and developing methods for ensuring that the standards are met.

The emphasis on quality assurance means that the practitioner, who is still having difficulty defining terms such as *problem, nursing need,* and *assessment,* is faced with an avalanche of new terms[1]. One asks what is quality, and how is it assured? Exploration of this question leads one into another set of terms: *outcomes, objectives, standards, efficiency, effectiveness, process,* and *structure* are some of the more common ones. It is not that nurses have not evaluated nursing care, nor had their practice evaluated, nor that they are totally unfamiliar with the termin-

ology. It is rather that the familiar terms are now being used in different contexts and at times with new meanings. Also, various authorities may define the terms differently. This chapter will attempt to clarify the meaning of the most commonly used terms.

QUALITY ASSURANCE

Quality assurance seems a reasonable beginning since all the other terms relate to it. One must ask first, what is quality? The American Heritage Dictionary defines quality as "a degree of excellence." In turn, excellence is described as "something in which a person or thing excels," and excel means "to be better than others; surpass; outdo." Thus, implied in the term *quality* is a value judgment about what constitutes excellence. Zimmer states that in nursing, "quality of care is defined by identifying the observable characteristics that depict the desired and valued degree of excellence and the expected observable variations. This becomes the standard for optimal achievable degree of excellence"[2]. The words *valued, optimal,* and *excellence,* all imply quality, and their use indicates that there exists a single standard against which nursing care characteristics can be measured and either accepted or rejected. This would simplify the process, but such widely accepted standards do not exist. Quality tends to exist in the eye and mind of the beholder, or in this case, of the practitioner.

Donabedian describes quality as a judgment of what constitutes good or bad work, with the good defined by standards set by leaders in the field at any given time[3]. These standards have either a normative or an empirical base. A normative base is "what is declared good by persons recognized as legitimate, authoritative sources of knowledge," while an empirical base is defined as "patterns of care observed in actual practice" in leading institutions, or a range of norms in a variety of agencies. It seems reasonable to assume, then, that quality is in large part dependent upon the standards set by the evaluators of care. Donabedian describes such standards as "operationalized definitions of the quality of care"[4].

The judgment as to what constitutes "good" care will be based, in part, on the sources of knowledge available to and used by the individuals or groups describing the characteristics of excellence in nursing care. Such resources as research facilities, libraries, and agencies with sophisticated clinical facilities and clinical specialists will all influence the decisions of standard setters. The impact of the observed practice and published norms of agencies would depend on the caliber of the agencies. Simply stated, an agency with unlimited access to the most current knowledge and practice in nursing may have a vastly different definition of quality than would an isolated agency with limited access to authoritative sources of knowledge and practice.

Any individual or group can describe quality nursing care and set standards for performance. However, in order to ensure that performance meets the standards, the individual or group must have the authority to influence practice. An obvious example of standards that are supported by power are the licensing laws of each state. However, others, such as the ANA's *Standards for Nursing Practice*, formulated by the Congress for Nursing Practice, must rely on acceptance by the individual nurse or the group that is setting standards in practice[5].

Since definition of quality alone may not affect practice or assure achievement of quality, another step is required. The American Heritage Dictionary defines *assurance* as "the act of making certain." This is a rather straightforward definition of a complex and difficult process. A quality assurance program has three components: (1) standards that describe quality, (2) a system for collecting information about the degree of achievement of the standards, and (3) an action to bring performance into line with the standards. In any quality assurance program, the first step is to determine the standards that are to be assured.

STANDARDS

Quality of care is expressed through statements of standards. A *standard* is defined as "an acknowledged measure of comparison for quantitative or qualitative value; criterion; norm." Since *criterion* is often used interchangeably with standard, the term needs to be defined. A *criterion* is "a standard on which a judgment can be based." Although *standard* and *criterion* are synonymous, in practice they are often defined somewhat differently, or one term is used as a subcategory of the other. For example, a broad statement of quality may be called a *standard* while a more specific statement describing a component of the standard is called a *criterion*. An example of this is Smith's statement that "standards are predetermined criteria for nursing care all patients have a right to expect"[6]. On the other hand, Ainsworth describes *criteria* as "the predetermined standards of care," and *standards* as "allowable deviations from the norm"[7]. The American Heritage Dictionary defines *norm* as a "pattern described as typical."

At this point, one might say that, in describing quality, there is an ultimate standard/criterion that describes either the highest level of achievement or the final stage in terms of a time sequence. Then, there is a series of more limited and/or more specific standards/criteria describing intermediate steps in achievement of the ultimate standard/criterion. Before illustrating the use of these terms in relation to a commonly occurring health care problem, two other terms need defining. A *criterion measure* is an item describing a degree of accomplishment of a standard/criterion. A *critical indicator* is a criterion measure essential to the accomplishment of the standard/criteria.

Example:
A newly diagnosed diabetic being discharged on 30 units NPH insulin daily would be expected by the time of discharge from the agency to meet the following standard/criteria. (This is a very limited one for demonstration purposes only.)

Standard/Criterion (*Ultimate*). The client/patient will be able to administer insulin to himself correctly and safely.

Sub Standard/Criterion (*Intermediate*). The client/patient will be able to verbalize the peak action of the insulin.

Criterion Measures
Patient can state time of peak in relation to time of administration.

States time in relation to the usual time of administration but not when this time is altered.

Unable to relate times of administration and peak.

The above criterion is a critical indicator because it is essential to achievement of the ultimate standard/criterion.

A Noncritical Indicator. The client/patient is able to verbalize the difference in action of oral diabetic agents and insulin.

Another term frequently used to describe standards is *indices. Indices* are a listing of series of items that constitute a whole. An example is provided by Zimmer, when she cites positive and negative indices of health for identification of outcomes, and by Phaneuf, who uses seven functions of nursing as indices of nursing practice[8, 9].

Norms describe ranges of accomplishment, and are usually based upon data collected on adequate populations or upon expert opinion derived from sufficient experience to indicate that the norms are typical. Norms may be stated in terms of levels of accomplishment at progressive stages in the solution of a health problem. They may also predict appropriate expectations for solution of health problems on the basis of the severity of the problem and its potential for solution. For example, when medicine can predict outcomes for an individual patient on the basis of statistics collected on a population of individuals with the same health problems and similar variables affecting recovery, norms are being used. Unlike medicine, nursing has few norms that can be used in developing standards.

All of the above are standards. Few, if any, standards are permanent or immutable. According to Donabedian, standards must be specified in "endless detail, reflecting the differences in situations, change in knowledge and the scope of provider responsibility"[10].

FRAMES OF REFERENCE FOR STANDARDS

Frames of reference describe the focus of a standard. In quality assurance programs, the frame of reference determines the data to be collected, and subsequently directs the action to be taken, if needed, to assure quality. The commonly accepted frames of reference for setting standards for the evaluation of the quality of health care are structure, process, and outcomes[11].

Structure

Structure deals with the characteristics of the care-providing system and is described as the environment by Bloch, and as resources by Zimmer[12,13]. Structure seems to be a sound word because it relates to the framework that provides support for the actual provision of care in any agency. Structure includes such disparate items as people, money, equipment, buildings, staffing policies, and educational resources. It has been for many years the major framework for evaluating care in health care agencies. Although somewhat discredited or omitted in current discussions of quality assurance, structure cannot be ignored. Aydelotte clearly establishes the relationship of one aspect of structure to the quality of nursing care when she states that "nurse staffing methodology should be an orderly systematic process, based upon sound rationale, applied to determine the number and kind of nursing personnel required to provide nursing care of a *predetermined standard* to a group of patients in a particular setting"[14]. When standards in the process and outcomes frames of reference are being set, the structure of the health care delivery agency must be assessed.

Structure involves both effectiveness and efficiency. *Effectiveness* can be defined as the degree to which an identified goal is achieved. *Efficiency* is basically the amount of effort (in terms of time, money, energy, etc.) needed to achieve the goal. In systems terms, effectiveness is concerned with output, while efficiency is concerned with input.

An example of this relationship is provided by del Bueno, who notes the relatively high degree of inefficiency exhibited in the orientation programs for recent graduates in their first position. She estimates that a period of up to six months is needed before they achieve competence (effectiveness). She defines *competence* as ability to meet the performance requirements of the position. In this instance, the output is competence and the input is the orientation and training programs, part of the structural frame of reference. She indicates that the structure, although effective (in terms of achieving the goal), is not efficient (in terms of time, money, and personnel). A large proportion of the time of administrators, who are concerned with devising structure to achieve desired standards of health care, is spent in balancing effectiveness and efficiency to identify the critical path, "the most efficient and effective system to produce a desired output or product with a given amount of resources"[15].

Process

The use of standards based on structure implies that if the structure is adequate, desirable goals will be achieved. Thus, employment of an adequate number of appropriately prepared practitioners should contribute significantly to the achievement of a high standard of care. However, the presence or absence of structural elements is not the only factor that determines the standard of care. The actual activities involved in providing care are crucial in determining the quality of care. These activities belong in the process frame of reference.

Process standards describe the behaviors of the nurse at the desired level of performance. These standards are most frequently couched in action terms, that is, "the nurse assesses...." or, "if the patient exhibits x symptoms, the nurse does this." An example of a broad or ultimate standard in the process frame of reference is provided by the published standards of the Congress for Nursing Practice[16]. More specific criteria can be found in Phaneuf's *Nursing Audit*[17].

Other process standards that are relatively new are those used in such practice areas as coronary care, intensive care, or primary care. In these areas, sets of standards variously called *regimens, protocols,* or *algorithms* are used. A *regimen*, and the closely related *protocol*, is "a systematic procedure of therapy," and an *algorithm* is described as a "step by step procedure and established pattern for the management of common problems"[18]. Such standards are described at length in Tucker et al., *Patient Care Standards*[19]. Although related to the traditional medical standing orders, these process standards afford the nurse a wider range of options and the opportunity for exercising greater judgment in selecting the appropriate action in providing care.

In all these standards, the focus is on what was planned for and with the patient and his family; what was done with, for, or to him; how it was done; and the quality of communication and recording that accompanied the activities. Despite the emphasis on nursing activities, process standards are not and should not be a mechanism for evaluating the quality of an individual practitioner's performance. Process standards describe a quality of nursing care provided usually by more than one practitioner and quite often by a team of nursing personnel of differing levels of competence. For the individual practitioner attempting to exercise quality control in direct patient care, the means standard described by Nicholls would be considered a process standard, for it describes nursing actions[20].

Outcomes

The third frame of reference is outcomes, which describe the results of nursing activity in terms of the change that occurs in the patient. The American Heritage Dictionary defines *outcome* as "a natural result; consequence." In other words, as a result of nursing actions or inactions there is or is not a change in the patient. Outcomes occur as a result of any planned or unplanned interaction between nurses and patients, and they may or may not be positive. In quality assurance programs, outcomes are usually stated in positive terms since the goal of such programs is the improvement of the client's health status.

Stevens believes that outcomes would be an "ideal" frame of reference if they could be based on the findings of sophisticated research that clearly identifies nursing's contribution to the outcome[21]. This basis for outcomes can only be used after a research-based body of knowledge establishes a clear cause and effect relationship between nursing intervention and changes in patient health.

The development of PSROs has encouraged nurses to attempt to identify outcomes in practice. Such activities may eventually lead to the identification of nursing norms for common health problems. In the context of these quality assurance programs, Zimmer defines *outcomes* as "an alteration in the health status of the patient caused by goal directed nursing care activities"[22]. The development of national norms, plus an increasing body of knowledge based on research, could serve as authoritative source material not only for quality assurance programs, but also for use in developing operational objectives for individual patient care. This raises the question: Aren't outcomes and objectives the same?

OUTCOMES-OBJECTIVES-GOALS

The American Heritage Dictionary defines a *goal* as "an end, objective," while its applicable definition of *objective* is "serving as a goal for a course of action." The terms are synonymous and are concerned with values. They describe desirable results of action and are projected into the future. They are used interchangeably, but also may be used differentially to specify time spans ("the long-range goal is...."; "the short-term objectives are...."). Others might state that "the long-range objective was achieved through the accomplishment of short-term goals." Or there may be broad or general goals and specific objectives. The practice of using only one term (for example, short- and long-range goals) increases the confusion.

In any case, objectives and/or goals describe a future result of a planned activity. While an objective/goal describes something that does not as yet exist, an outcome describes something that has already happened. In quality assurance programs, outcomes are designed specifically to be used as standards for evaluating nursing care that has already occurred. An outcome can be used as a goal for nursing care *only* when an adjective is ued to modify it ("the desirable outcome for this patient would be....").

Is there danger in confusing the terms *objectives* and *outcomes*? It seems relatively easy to transfer outcome criteria for the evaluation of the quality of care to standardized nursing care plans. However, outcomes are developed for populations of patients with frequently occurring problems. Although the criteria may be applicable to a selected population of patients and could be converted into objectives, such criteria might not be applicable for care for large numbers of other patients with somewhat different characteristics. Furthermore, the criteria are designed to "monitor critical events" and not all aspects of the nursing care. Thus, using outcomes as objectives could lead to the development of standardized care plans that are relatively inflexible and which would be inappropriate for patients with different

problems or when used without exercise of judgment in solving individuals' unique problems. The development and use of outcomes as standards for evaluating nursing care *post facto* should contribute significantly to the construction of an authoritative body of standards that the practitioner could refer to in setting operational objectives for individual care.

At this point, the greatest emphasis seems to be on the outcomes frame of reference—on the premise that it is results that count. If outcomes are positive, then the structure and process frames of reference do not seem as important. If, however, outcomes are not meeting expectations, then the structure and process frames of reference assume greater importance. Bloch contends that "only an evaluation that encompasses both process and outcome has the potential for great impact on the quality of care"[23].

An important factor in the selection of the frame of reference is the relationship between effectiveness and efficiency in the data collection component of the quality assurance process. The goal is to devise a data collection system that is reliable, valid, and efficient in the use of time and staff, and which will provide information to guide action to ensure achievement of standards. The common approach is to use some form of audit.

AUDIT

To audit is "to examine or verify." The process of examining can be either concurrent or retrospective. It can be used for all three frames of reference. For example, an examiner could audit an aspect of the structure of a nursing unit by collecting a random sample of staffing patterns over a six-month period. This would be a retrospective audit, for it would use records to collect data about past performance. From the collected data, a conclusion could be drawn as to whether the actual staffing met the pre-established standard. In such cases, more accurate data may be collected in retrospective than in concurrent audit since the data cannot be manipulated as easily with random retrospective data collection.

When process is evaluated the audit can be concurrent, as when nursing practice is observed and measured against preestablished criteria such as the Wandelt Quality Patient Care Scale (QualPaCS), or other agency-developed standards[24]. Generally, concurrent audit of process calls for the use of professional judgment. Such programs require the time of nursing staff, who are removed from their usual nursing assignment to do the audit; it is often considered a relatively expensive audit.

Retrospective process audit is described by Phaneuf as "a method for evaluating quality of care through appraisal of the nursing process as it is reflected in the patient care records for discharged patients"[25]. In this type of audit, specified behaviors are described under seven functions of nursing. The behaviors are converted into questions for which the examiner seeks answers in the patient's record. This type of audit requires professional judgment, but may be less time-consuming and thus less expensive.

Since outcomes are the result of action, audit of outcomes must by definition be retrospective. However, the focus of the data collection is on patient responses rather than nurse behaviors. In this frame of reference, it has been proposed that if the criteria are described clearly, and nurses develop habits of recording clearly, completely, and accurately, professional judgment will not be needed in auditing records. This will reduce the involvement of professional nurses in the data collection process, but not in the setting of standards.

In many agencies, more than one frame of reference is used; in addition to the patient and his record, sources for data include the Kardex, Nursing Care Plans, and observed practice. An example of the use of concurrent audit that involves all three frames of reference is provided in Carter et al., *Standards of Nursing Care*[26]. For the individual nurse, continuous, concurrent data collection is necessary to ensure outcomes that meet individual, professional, and agency standards.

ACTION—THE ASSURANCE OF STANDARDS

It would be ridiculous to define the term *act*, but it is necessary to identify what kind of action is initiated, the arenas in which action takes place, and who initiates it. If the audit is initiated and conducted by an accrediting agency, the actions might include warnings, consultation, and as a last resort, removal of accreditation. If the administration of a nursing department in an agency initiates the audit and the action, any one of several actions might be instituted, including: review of practice by concurrent audit, counseling, assessment of the adequacy of resources, provision of training, and disciplinary action. If responsibility for the audit is in the hands of a committee of practitioners elected by their peers, then the actions might include such things as educating their peers about deficiencies in practice, recommending policy changes to administration, and identifying learning needs. Where standards fall below levels acceptable to nurses as individuals or as a group, they may exert pressure on an agency to alter practices that are considered unsafe or inadequate.

SUMMARY

Quality assurance is a relatively easy concept to grasp. It involves the description of the level of quality desired and feasible, and a system for ensuring its achievement. In practice, it becomes complex because of the need to elaborate levels of quality and to devise appropriate data collection systems. It is further complicated by the manner in which the terminology is used.

The nursing practitioner needs to develop a set of terms describing the process of quality assurance that can be used in practice. A good grasp of the process makes comprehension of new terms or terms used in a different manner much easier. Quality assurance is not just the concern of administrators; it should be the concern of the nurse, who can be assigned to participate in all three components of the process: standard setting, data collection, and action to meet standards. Regardless of participation in departmental programs, the practicing nurse is responsible for setting operational standards in direct patient care. To do this, the nurse needs to understand the process and terminology of quality assurance.

REFERENCES

1. Bloch, D. Some crucial terms in nursing. What do they mean? *Nurs. Outlook*, Vol. 22, No. 11, 1974, p. 689.
2. Zimmer, M. Quality assurance for outcomes of Nursing care. *Nurs. Clin. North Am.*, Vol. 9, No. 2, 1974, p. 307.
3. Donabedian, A. Promoting quality through evaluating the process of patient care. *Med. Care*, Vol. 6, No. 3, 1968, p. 182.
4. Donabedian, A. 1968, p. 187.
5. Congress for Nursing Practice, *Standards for Nursing Practice*, Kansas City: American Nurses Association, 1973.
6. Smith, D. Writing objectives as a nursing practice skill. *Am. J. Nurs.*, Vol. 71, No. 2, 1971, p. 319.
7. Ainsworth, T.J. "The American Hospital Association Quality Control Program, The American Medical Association's Peer Review Program, and Social Security Amendments for Quality Assurance," in *Proceedings of an Institute for Quality Assurance for Nursing Care*. Kansas City: American Nurses Association and American Hospital Association, 1973, p. 72.
8. Zimmer, M.J. "Quality Assurance for Nursing Care" in *Proceedings of an Institute for Quality Assurance for Nursing Care*. Kansas City: American Nurses Association and American Hospital Association, 1973, p. 14.
9. Phaneuf, M.C. *The Nursing Audit: A Profile for Excellence*. New York: Appleton-Century-Crofts, 1972, p. 16.
10. Donabedian, A. 1968, p. 182.
11. Donabedian, A. Some crucial issues in evaluating the quality of nursing care. Part II. *Am. J. Pub. Hlth.*, Vol. 59, No. 10, 1969, p. 1833.
12. Bloch, D. 1974, p. 257.
13. Zimmer, M.J. 1974, p. 308.
14. Aydelott, M.K. *Nursing Staffing Methodology*. Washington, D.C.: U.S. Dept. of HEW (No. NIH 73-433), 1973, p. 3.
15. delBueno, D.J. The cost of competency. *J. Nurs. Admin.*, Vol. 5, No. 8, 1975, p. 16.
16. Congress for Nursing Practice 1973.
17. Phaneuf, M.C. 1972, chap. 3.
18. Berni, R. and Ready, H. *Problem Oriented Record Implementation, Allied Health Peer Review.* St. Louis: C.V. Mosby, 1974, p. 61.
19. Tucker, S.M. et al. *Patient Care Standards*. St. Louis: C.V. Mosby, 1975.
20. Nicholls, M.E. Quality control in patient care. *Am. J. Nurs.*, Vol. 74, No. 3, 1974, p. 456ff.
21. Stevens, B. Analysis of trends in nursing care management. *J. Nurs. Admin.*, Vol. 2, No. 6, 1972, p. 13.
22. Zimmer, M.J. A model for evaluating nursing care. *Hospitals,* Vol. 48, 1974, p. 91.
23. Bloch, D. Evaluation of nursing care in terms of process and outcomes: Issues in research and quality assurance. *Nurs. Res.*, Vol. 24, No. 4, 1975, p. 258.
24. Wandelt, M.A. and Ager, J. *Quality Patient Care Scale*. Detroit: College of Nursing, Wayne State University, 1970.
25. Phaneuf, M.C. 1972, p. 15.
26. Carter, J.H. et al. *Standards of Nursing Care: A Guide for Evaluation*. New York: Springer, 1972.

UNIT II

FACTORS AFFECTING NURSING STANDARDS

Introduction

There are many forces and factors that bear directly on the nurse as she formulates and implements standards of care at the practice level. When Ms. Jones, R.N., establishes a nurse-patient relationship with Mr. Smith, she contracts to provide nursing care for him. Because the factors that affect the nurse are diverse and she may exercise control over only a few of them at any given time, the quality of care Mr. Smith receives will reflect the impact of these factors. The way in which the individual nurse responds to the various factors will determine her standard of nursing care. Thus, each nurse's standards in practice are to some degree unique. It is the decision to do or not do something or to give priority to one behavior over another that, in reality, sets the standard for the nursing care an individual patient receives. A given nurse's standards could be identified if one could observe her responses to the various factors over a period of time. Each nurse's pattern of responses tend to be unique. Because each nurse's standards are unique, a nursing department should develop inservice education

programs and set up quality assurance programs.

The factors affecting nurses who set standards in practice, particularly in hospital practice, that appear most relevant are addressed in this unit.

Nicholls's chapter introduces the range of factors and examines the ones most likely to influence the nurse as she sets operational standards for the direct care of patients.

An increasingly strong voice in the field of standard setting for health care is that of the consumer. Carnegie's chapter presents two documents that deal specifically with consumers' rights. Although nursing has articulated its concern for patients' rights, evidence supporting this concern must be supplied at the operational level.

The standards of the nurse at the operational level should be consistent with those of the department of nursing in which she practices. Moore's chapter speaks with exceptional clarity to the need for a precise statement of a nursing department's philosophy, purpose, and objectives to provide clear direction for nurses in the department.

The use of outcome criteria as standards for evaluating nursing care in quality assurance programs is relatively new. Throughout the country, many nurses are involved in setting outcome criteria for the patient populations they serve. Zimmer's chapter explains what outcome criteria are, how they are developed and used in nursing quality assurance programs.

Stevens's chapter is aimed at the director of nursing service and describes how quality assurance programs can be initiated by the department of nursing. While not speaking specifically to the nurse at the practice level, it provides effective orientation to several approaches to quality assurance. It is particularly effective in explaining the difference between the structure and process frames of reference for setting standards as well as the difference between task analysis and other types of quality control programs.

Chapter 6

Factors Affecting Nursing Standards at the Practice Level

Marion E. Nicholls

The individual nurse's standards are constantly being influenced by a number of factors. Modifications in standards for nursing care begin almost immediately after graduation from nursing school. The impact of reality on standards acquired as a student is described by Kramer as "reidentification of self from one who is a 'budding professional nurse working in utopia' to one who sees herself as a 'budding professional working in the imperfect, sometimes illogical, reality of today' "[1]. In this "imperfect, sometimes illogical, reality," the nurse constantly sets and re-sets standards for patient care. Donabedian describes this as a characteristic of standards. They must be "specified in endless detail, reflecting changing situations, change in knowledge and scope of provider responsibility"[2].

Few people think in terms of "setting a standard." Concern for standards is usually indicated imprecisely by such statements as, "How can I give good care without adequate staff?" Or, "You can really give good care on that unit."

The sum total of what the nurse believes are desirable patient outcomes and the priorities she assigns to nursing activities describe that nurse's unique standard of nursing care. This standard is an expression of the quality of care that this individual can achieve at this time, and the quality is influenced by many factors. Awareness of these factors can help the practitioner set meaningful standards for individual practice and participate more effectively in the development of departmental standards for nursing care.

In 1968, Donabedian wrote that the description of what is "good" in professional practice is provided by leaders in the field; today, there is pressure on practitioners as well as leaders to participate in the standard-setting process [3].

In the past it was generally accepted that educators rather than practitioners set the standards for nursing care. There has been an increasing shift of responsibility for standard setting from educators to practitioners. In part, this is due to the increased number of nurses functioning in expanded roles that have stimulated examination of traditional standards for practice. In part, it reflects the increasing emphasis on the practitioner's obligation to set standards, as indicated in the ANA statement, "It is the belief of the American Nurses' Association that practitioners of nursing bear the primary responsibility and accountability for the quality of nursing care clients/patients receive"[4]. Zimmer believes in the ability of nurses at the direct care level to participate in setting standards: "Practicing nurses who have had good experience in the care of specific patient populations know the desired and relevant patient health outcomes"[5].

There is an urgent need to define nursing, set standards, and demonstrate that the standards can be met. Professional Standards Review Organization (PSRO) legislation has challenged health care providers to produce programs that will meet these requirements. Since the definition of nursing and how it shall be practiced is at stake, all nurses should be involved in the decision making. Limitations on the time available in which to accomplish this requires participation of large numbers of nurses at all levels, but particularly nurses practicing at the direct care level.

Accompanying the need to define nursing care for PSROs is the need to identify nursing's contribution to health care in order to meet the onslaught of new "health workers" seeking to carve their own niche in the expanding and, for some, profitable health care field. In order to avoid playing the role of dog in the manger, nursing must examine its role and determine how well it meets society's needs.

To fulfill a professional role, the nurse must function on four levels of standard setting. First, and perhaps most important, is the nurse's responsibility for the standard of the care she provides or directs. Second, the quality of nursing care provided on specific units and the nursing department of an agency should be the concern of all practitioners in the agency. Nurses should make

known their support of sound practice. Willingness to support or condone unsafe practice in a unit, department, or agency is not professional behavior. Third, a professional nurse should be concerned with the level of health care, and particularly nursing care, in her community. The nurse in an acute care agency should also be concerned about the minimum standards of nursing care practiced in a nursing home. Individual involvement may be carried out through a professional organization, but all nurses should support standards of nursing care that are acceptable to the nursing community. If nursing fails to assume responsibility for setting standards, it will relinquish this right to other groups in the health care delivery system. Fourth, if national nursing standards are to be authoritative standards in practice, then the practitioner should be a knowledgeable critic, if not always an active participant, in the setting of those standards. In Figure 1, some factors that have impact on standards set at the practice level are identified. To avoid assigning precedence to any particular set of factors, we have placed the six factors in a circle.

FACTORS IN SOCIETY

A nurse would have to be grossly uninformed to be unaware of society's deep concern over the problems of health care. Society's changing needs, values, and requirements in relation to health care are mirrored in numerous articles, books, television programs, and various legislative programs designed to solve problems in health care delivery. As a member of society, the nurse shares these concerns; as a nurse, she must be responsive to society's needs and concerns.

Service professions exist at the will of society and are influenced by the changes in the society they serve. Society and the pro-

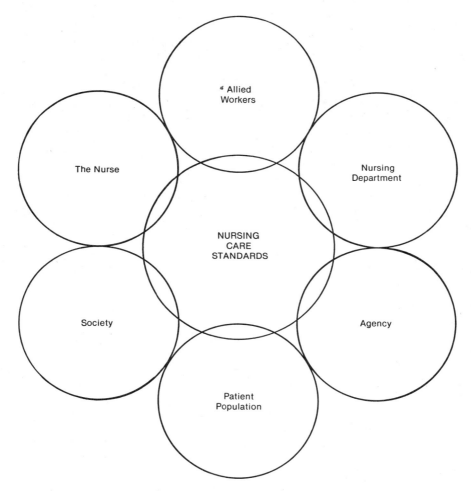

FIGURE 1. SOURCES OF FACTORS AFFECTING NURSING CARE STANDARDS AT THE PRACTICE LEVEL

fession interact to determine mutual goals. This is not to say that these goals are always clearly articulated, or that vested interests (in society and in the professions) do not sometimes try to assume the major role in setting goals. For example, the medical profession prefers specialized practice in urban areas near medical centers, while society increasingly demands a more equitable distribution of medical services. Recent proposals for national health insurance bills have frequently included measures that attempt to ensure better distribution of medical services.

The American public has undergone a revolution of rising expectations in which the definition of health has been expanded to include, in addition to the absence of disease, "the assurance of energy, vitality, even perpetual youth and beauty"[6]. Perhaps not surprisingly, much of the public's expectations are based on the almost miraculous technical discoveries of the past century.

Along with the expectation of positive health, society, is demanding the right to participate, individually and collectively in decision-making processes in health care. The consumer of health care, while continuing to value scientific medicine, places increasing emphasis on the manner of delivery. He wants it delivered in a "respectful and dignified manner at a price he can afford; increasingly, he wants to know what is going on and why"[7]. Attempts to meet society's needs include the development of Regional Planning Groups, Health Maintenance Organizations, and PSROs; more directly affecting nursing is the development of the expanded roles for nurses such as primary care nurses and nurse practitioners.

The public's fiscal commitment to health care is enormous. An estimated $105 billion was spent in 1974; the government—federal, state and local—assumed 37 percent of the bill while the private sector paid the remaining 63 percent. However, society is increasingly critical of the value of the services and products received for this expenditure. It is reasonable to expect a continued close scrutiny of all health programs and services.

What impact does the public's commitment to health care have on the standards set by the practicing nurse? First, a public deeply concerned with health is becoming more knowledgeable about health, disease, and therapy. The practitioner's standards for nursing care should reflect this trend in two ways: (1) any nursing standard must be supported by sound rationale that is capable of interpretation to the consumer, and (2) the standard must reflect an effort to provide the public with improved health. To a public increasingly sophisticated in health care, ambiguous nursing standards can only be interpreted as evidence of ignorance. In those areas where nursing has been man-

dated to function, the nurse will be expected to speak authoritatively. To do this, practitioners must keep their knowledge and skills up to date in relevant practice areas.

On a community level, the nurse practitioner has an obligation to participate in community efforts to establish health care standards and particularly standards for nursing care in the health care delivery system. Failure to participate in setting standards for nursing care and tacit support of unsound care leads to a lack of confidence in nurses as authoritative health professionals. The nurse must become articulate in communicating nursing standards to the community so that society's decisions will reflect these standards.

In setting standards for care at the practice level, we must recognize that the cost of nursing care will be a significant factor in the public's evaluation of the profession's contribution to health care. Standards for nursing care that do not reflect the economic realities of the community will not be acceptable. Throughout the country, PSROs are being organized among physicians to "judge the medical necessity for care rendered within health care institutions in accordance with professional standards"[9]. Similar standards are expected to evolve for all health professionals with the passage of some form of national health insurance. Thus, practicing nurses must help determine the standards that differentiate the quality of care provided by or under the direction of professional nurses from the quality of the care provided by less expensive workers.

Another consideration will be the need to determine if a desirable standard of nursing care can be achieved at a lower cost to the consumer. For example, if it could be proven that a more effective patient teaching program, even one entailing a longer hospitalization, reduced chances of readmission, it might well be accepted by the public as an economy. In this case, a high standard of nursing care could result in a long-range reduction in cost to the public.

Society's expectations of nursing have been conditioned by popular movies and television programs that usually cast the nurse as a "girl Friday" to a more commanding male figure, doctor, medic, or even ambulance driver. In order to increase the stature of the male star, the nurse is portrayed as requiring an order for every action, implying an inability to make even simple decisions.

Nursing has to some extent contributed to the negative public image. It has failed to develop "an autonomously effective practice" that is recognized as worthwhile by either the public or other professionals[10]. Recently, nurses have been gaining increased respect in a variety of ways. Their expanded role has provided them with an opportunity to demonstrate new skills and decision-making abilities to the public. Small but increasing numbers of nurses have been entering private practice and others have become politically active, providing the public with a different view of the profession.

Nurses must be more assertive in identifying autonomous nursing practice and in setting and communicating standards in whatever agency they practice. The authority for setting the standards must derive from the effectiveness of the nursing care, not from administrative acquiscence or through pseudo-medical competence. Until such authority is established, the public's expectations of nursing may be less than what the profession expects of itself.

In two very specific ways, society expresses its expectation of nursing. The first is through the legal definition of nursing accepted in Nurse Practice Acts. The second is its willingness to authorize third party payment for independent nursing practice.

Legal definitions of nursing tend to be rather general, but they usually do indicate the degree of autonomy granted to practice nursing. In some states where the expanded role of the nurse has been acknowledged, supervision by physicians and others has been incorporated into the licensing procedure, raising questions of autonomy in practice[11]. The New York State definition permits considerable autonomy in practice if the nurse is willing and able to use it.

The practice of the profession of nursing as a registered professional nurse is defined as diagnosing and treating human responses to actual or potential health problems through such services as casefinding, health teaching, health counseling, and provision of care supportive to or restorative of life and well-being, and executing medical regimens prescribed by a licensed or otherwise legally authorized physician or dentist. A nursing regimen shall be consistent with and shall not vary from any existing medical regimen[12].

Society validates a profession's contribution to the public welfare by authorizing third party payment for services rendered. In nursing care delivery, such legislation would open the way for direct contracting between the nurse and patient for nursing care. Authorization of third party payment will permit increased independent private practice for nurses and direct nursing referrals from agency to agency. As long as referral for nursing service requires a medical order, a nurse's autonomy to set nursing standards for care is open to question.

FACTORS RELATED TO PATIENTS

These factors are perhaps those most familiar to nurse practitioners and need the least elaboration. Patients are members of society and share many of the expectations of society. In a society as diverse as ours, assessment of individual patients is essential because age, culture, and financial status may create individual differences in expectations about nursing care. Nursing literature attests to the profession's long-established concern with individualization of nursing care. Nurses are also accustomed to examining the composition of their patient population and identifying the most commonly occurring health problems. The practicing nurse balances daily the needs of the individual patients and those of the group of patients for whom she is responsible. The question is: To what extent do nurses identify appropriate achievable standards of nursing care for these groups of patients? Is it reasonable to expect that nurses caring primarily for convalescent, postoperative patients can achieve an excellent standard of care for a critically ill patient requiring sophisticated technical care when, for lack of an available bed in the Intensive Care Unit, the patient stays on the surgical unit? What happens to other patients while efforts are bent to meet the needs of the critically ill patient? On the other hand, should standards for nursing care require that a nurse in an Intensive Care Unit devote much time to teaching?

What is the expected standard of care when the patient population represents a veritable alphabet soup of diagnoses and therapies? For the "float" or "relief" nurse, patient populations are constantly changing, often too rapidly to permit anything more than superficial assessment of needs. In all of these instances, practicing nurses are more likely to set standards for care on a reactive rather than a problem-solving basis. Current efforts to identify desirable nursing outcomes for populations of patients with commonly occurring problems show promise of developing some standards for these populations on a more rational basis. Certainly, each patient in a given population has

the right to expect at least the standard for nursing care received by other members of the same population. Hopefully, with more clearly enunciated standards at the practice level, nurses may be able to influence the composition of patient populations to achieve more equitable nursing care standards for patients with similar health care problems or therapeutic requirements.

Along with the right to receive appropriate and equitable nursing care, patients are seeking other rights. Carnegie lists the rights included in the American Hospital Association Patients' Bill of Rights and in the National League for Nursing's document, "What People Can Expect of a Modern Nursing Service." The Patient's Bill of Rights focuses on the role of the physician and the hospital in ensuring the patient's rights to information and participation in decision making, while the League for Nursing's document bases the amount of information the nurse may convey to the patient on the doctor's willingness to share information with the patient and to involve the patient in decision making. Nurses may be faced with increasingly militant patients and families who will demand information physicians are reluctant to give. They may need to identify more clearly the amount of information the patient needs to be able to achieve the highest level of health care after discharge and to communicate this information requirement effectively to physicians.

The nurse practitioner, who subscribes to the belief that patients should not be included in research projects without their full knowledge and agreement, may find herself in the uncomfortable position of having either to challenge a researcher or to inform a patient about his involvement in research or to allow the project to proceed without interference. Failure to act would indicate that the nurse was ignoring at least one standard of nursing care related to human dignity. Alert, informed nurses who support professional standards at the practice level are the patients' greatest resource for retaining their rights and for maintaining their dignity as individuals.

FACTORS IN THE AGENCY

When applying for a position, the nurse is only generally aware of the purpose of the agency. For example, the major purpose of a large medical center that is part of a university may be viewed as service to the community. This may be one of its purposes, but it usually ranks below two other purposes: education of health personnel, particularly doctors and research. The first two purposes affect the care of patients within the agency in many ways. The nurse will often find that patients receive the latest treatments and medicines and have access to a well-prepared group of resource people. However, the emphasis on learning may lead to unnecessary patient transfers, interference by learners in nursing programs designed to meet nursing goals, and erratic staffing patterns designed to meet the needs of learners, not patients. A nurse applying to a well-appointed nursing home with a beautifully stated purpose, may discover, if it is a proprietary agency, that its overriding purpose is to make a profit.

In order to set realistic standards, the nurse should attempt to determine an agency's real purpose or purposes. After determining the agency's purpose, the nurse can decide what level of nursing standards the agency can reasonably be expected to support. The practitioner should consider whether the agency's standard of nursing care is so low that it endangers the public. In many instances, the standard falls somewhere between desirable and unsafe, and each nurse's unique standards will dictate which agency is acceptable and which is not.

If the agency's achievable standards fall within a range acceptable to the nurse, or if there is a real possibility for improvement of unacceptable standards, the nurse would find the agency suitable for practice.

An agency's resources have a vital impact upon its ability to achieve its goals. The impact of resources on the setting and meeting of standards is so obvious that it seems hardly to need discussion. Yet, in nursing, it is a factor that is often ignored when standards are being set and nursing care evaluated. The level of financial support for nursing care is crucial in determining the quality of care. The availability of funds for adequate staffing, appropriate equipment, and access to other well-staffed and well-equipped supportive departments cannot ensure a high standard of nursing care, but the absence of these resources can have a negative effect on the quality of nursing care. Nurses tend to set a single standard for nursing care regardless of the resources available to an agency. Limited resources can be compensated for by better organization, creativity in the use of resources, and careful attention to priorities. After these means have been exhausted, then existing resources play a crucial role in the standard of nursing care that can be achieved. When resources consistently fall below the level necessary to achieve an acceptable standard of nursing care, the nurse has an obligation to attempt to change the situation.

In any agency, the formal agency structure is the channel for communicating concern over standards. All health care agencies have a bureaucratic structure, a hierarchical arrangement of individuals and departments. Although informal channels of influence may exist, power and influence move along the formal organizational line. The placement of the director of nursing in the hierarchy is often an indicator of the degree of influence this person can exert on policy and, more importantly, on budget decisions. In general, the further removed the director of nursing is from the agency's policy-making level, the less real control nurses can expect to have over the standards of nursing care.

The nurse's freedom to participate in setting standards at the practice level may be determined by the administration's management philosophy. In a rigid, hierarchical, authoritarian structure, autonomy is limited and nursing standards are often restricted by task-oriented procedures and policies. A more decentralized organization presents nurses with more autonomy and less structured practice. Nurses in the more decentralized organizations are expected to set new standards that are relevant to changing roles in nursing practice. These standards are measured against the question, "Does the standard contribute to patient welfare?" If the practitioner cannot formulate nursing standards independently, then the standards for nursing practice are set by the medical or other health care providers in the agency. Nurses able to assess patients' nursing needs in unstructured units and capable of supporting their nursing interventions with sound rationale can establish nursing standards that are likely to be accepted by other members of the health care team.

Intimately tied into the nurse's ability to set standards is the assigned role of nursing. Generally, when other people's roles impinge on our own, we view their role in terms of how it makes our role more rational. For example, administrators may view the primary function of nursing as support of the agency and the administrator; the doctor may view the nurse's primary role as supportive to the medical regimen and the doctor; while the nurse may view the administrator's role as supportive to nursing and may view the doctor as a colleague. Since both the administrator and doctor enjoy more power

in health care agencies, their view of the nurse's role is likely to be the predominant one. If the administrator and/or doctor do not see nursing as having an independent role, then they may given nurses very little time to practice nursing.

When the largest number of staff are technicians and the only professional nurses are serving primarily as administrators and medical assistants, nursing standards will reflect the technical and physical care orientation of the actual deliverers of care. The standard for nursing care tends to level off at the standards of the best prepared practitioner actually providing nursing care. The degree to which nurses can fulfill an independent nursing role is related in large part to the strength and direction of the nursing department administration.

FACTORS IN THE DEPARTMENT OF NURSING

Donovan believes that nursing service administration has "not yet reached maturity," and cites lack of proper educational preparation for nursing service administrators, limited numbers of trained hospital administrators, and the traditional "doer" rather than "thinker" role of nurses. As an example of the ineffectiveness of nursing service administration, she cites its lack of protest over the "dissipation of nursing that derives from nurses doing the work of so many departments of the hospital"[13]. In most instances, the director of nursing has a powerful role in setting and maintaining standards of nursing care in the agency.

The director of nursing's philosophy of nursing, of management, and of the role of the nurse will be crucial in determining policy that governs the department of nursing. It is well known that people in positions of authority tend to surround themselves with subordinates whose beliefs and/or performance are supportive of their own. This applies to the selection of directors of nursing by agency administrators. An agency administrator who feels that nursing should have little or no independent role would not hire a nursing administrator whose expressed views and past performance reflect a strong belief in the existence of such a role. It is advisable that the nursing director be largely in agreement with the administrator's views, because the functioning of the department of nursing will be expected to reflect those views.

As well as being an agency administrator, the director of nursing is also a member of the nursing profession and is exposed to pressure from the profession to establish and maintain standards set by the profession. This pressure comes from many sources: professional organizations, the agency nursing staff, and accrediting bodies. The director must interpret agency policy to the staff and at the same time interpret nursing standards to agency administrators. Evidence indicates that directors of nursing have succeeded more often in interpreting agency policy than in interpreting nursing.

The nursing department's standards for nursing care and for nursing practice are expressed in a variety of ways. They are communicated through statements of department purpose and objectives, through the policies and procedures governing the department, through job descriptions, through inservice education programs, and through criteria set for nursing care and nursing practice evaluation programs.

When looking at the stated purpose and objectives of an agency, the practitioner would do well to realize that many nursing administrators find ambiguity useful. Vague statements about philosophy and objectives are generally accepted by both agency administrators and accrediting visitors as appropriate, and do not commit the nursing department to any specific course of action.

The practitioner who attempts to meet the standards implied in these statements may find little administrative support or reward for her efforts.

In assessing the standards of a department of nursing, the nurse will find the following factors relevant. (1) Is the department's statement about philosophy and objectives clear and specific? If so, it may well represent the real intentions of the department, because such statements can be challenged and performance can be measured against the stated intent. Does the job description focus on nursing rather than non-nursing activities, describe role expectations, and reflect the degree of autonomy given to staff nurses? Answers to such questions are indicators of the department's expectations about the participation of staff nurses in standard setting. Expectations about the quality of nursing care can be judged by the availability of clinical nurse specialists and an active inservice education department.

(2) The existence and type of Peer Review Program is another important consideration. The American Nurses' Association defines peer review as "the process by which registered nurses actively engaged in the practice of nursing, appraise the quality of nursing care in a given situation in accordance with established standards of practice"[14]. The practitioner should be aware of the standards that are used and the definition of the term *peer*. The nurse should ask: "What are the standards?" and "Who sets them?" Clearly delineated standards can be supportive to the practicing nurse. While poorly defined or inadequate standards may not limit the practitioner, they do not provide adequate support for practice. The ambiguity of such standards leaves them open to interpretations that allow assignment of inadequate resources while placing legal responsibility for the standards of nursing care on the shoulders of the practicing

nurse. As damaging as ambiguous standards are, the opposite rigid, task-oriented standards permit little autonomy and encourage fragmenting of care. Equally harmful are nursing care standards that equate organization activities with nursing activities. For example, standards that determine the competence of the nurse on the basis of her skills in ordering supplies or other clerical activities indicate that the agency will misuse its nursing manpower.

The agency's definition of the term *peer* should be clear and comprehensible. Peers can be described as coworkers having equal standing in the activity in which they are engaged. Zimmer describes a group consisting of a head nurse, a staff nurse, and a clinical specialist involved in providing care to a specific patient population as a peer group [15]. A peer group composed of administrative supervisors and faculty formed to develop standards for a specific population of patients with whom they have little contact should perhaps be challenged. On the other hand, practitioners may be too limited in experience, unchallenged by recent learning, and too reluctant to make changes to be effective in developing standards for practice. The use of consultants in developing standards should help a nursing department evaluate the effectiveness of its peer review program.

A nursing staff that is able to set standards, participate in peer review programs, and effect changes can be a potent agent for elevating standards of practice. Ramphal states that effective peer review provides "collective strength in decision making which would make nursing, as an organized service, less vulnerable to non-nurse decisions about the ways in which nurses shall practice"[16].

In the setting of standards, an important source of support for the practicing nurse is the pattern of organization and staffing of nursing units. Organizational patterns such as case method or primary nursing, which require professional nurse involvement in all phases of nursing care, are most supportive. Primary nursing encourages nurses to assume responsibility for the setting of operational standards for nursing care. Functional nursing and some forms of team nursing organization may be less supportive. Functional organization, while encouraging efficiency in task accomplishment, discourages autonomous nursing planning and standard setting. Team nursing, although designed to provide a high standard of nursing care by arranging for professional nurses to lead other nursing staff in providing care, often degenerates into a form of functional nursing organization.

FACTORS EMANATING FROM OTHER HEALTH CARE PROVIDERS

Davidson points out the interdependence of professions in the health care field and the "pervasive dependence" of the patient acts as a "connecting factor in maintaining the institutional configuration and the common cause"[17]. However, competition for authority, resources, and even physical space have tended to create something less than a united effort and an effective team. Instead, it has encouraged professional and other health care workers to grapple for their piece of the pie and view others as competitors rather than teammates.

Rosasco supports the need for nursing to "identify, to describe, and to categorize their practice so that other professionals, as well as the public, will know what nursing is"[18]. She further cites the need for acknowledgment by institutions and other professionals that nursing practice is not the provision of services to the "institution and other members of the health team, but rather the provision of service to patients"[19]. Nursing's ambiguous role causes the director of nursing and the staff nurse alike to accept non-nursing duties and obligations. As a direct outcome, they may receive criticism for poor performance of tasks for which neither is prepared and also for poor nursing care provided while they were doing someone else's work.

What are some indicators of the attitudes of other health team members toward nursing? One indicator is the number and kinds of functions totally unrelated or marginally related to nursing care asked of nursing by other departments. One common example is the amount of clerical work assigned to meet the needs of doctors, laboratories, central supply, and the financial office. Another indicator may be the degree of encroachment of other health care workers into areas of practice commonly considered nursing practice. For example, in many extended care facilities a whole range of workers have claimed many nursing functions as their responsibility; in such situations, nursing's role is defined as largely maintaining and nursing jobs are assigned primarily to practical nurses and attendants. In such a setting a nurse would need to struggle to set standards for nursing care above the maintenance level. At the other end of the spectrum, primary care nurse practitioners may need to fight to retain a nursing role when physicians' expectations push them into the "little doctor" role.

The practicing nurse must assess the attitudes of fellow health team members toward nursing. If the role assigned to nursing is not congruent with the achievement of acceptable nursing care standards, nurses should try to change the attitude of the team members or make a decision about remaining in the agency. Such a decision would not be easy, but is necessary if nursing is to provide quality care to the public.

Nurses should describe, delineate, and demonstrate what nursing is to other members of the health team. At the same time, nursing should set and interpret standards for the nursing care that is provided in conjunction with care given by other health care workers. Ideally, the standards for the care of a given patient should be an amalgam of the standards of all the health care providers on the team responsible for the patient's care. Although reality may not reach this ideal, there is standard setting involved in health team planning for patient care. If nursing fails to provide effective input into such planning for patient care, it will leave the task of setting nursing standards to other health care providers. The degree to which the practicing nurse is able, willing, and expected by other team members to set nursing standards will have a direct impact on the quality of the standards set.

FACTORS IN THE PRACTICING NURSE

If one could assume that all nurses approach nursing care with the same goals and expertise, then this chapter would not be needed. However, nurses come from different backgrounds and display considerable variation in knowledge, skill, and values. Since it is our premise that it is the practicing nurse who, in the final analysis, determines the quality of care received by the patient, we must look at the factors affecting the individual nurse.

There is a veritable smorgasbord of educational programs, all accredited, to prepare the prospective nurse for licensure. There are baccalaureate, associate degree, and diploma programs. The curricula tend to be so unique to each institution that students have difficulty transferring from one institution to another. They also find it difficult if not impossible without testing and/or repetition of courses, to transfer from one type of program to another. Despite at least one common goal (preparation for licensure to practice nursing) each program determines its own philosophy and the nursing process that will be taught to its students.

What does this mean for the new graduate who is beginning practice? It seems obvious that at least in the beginning of practice, the definition of quality nursing care will be influenced by the nurse's educational preparation.

Diploma programs have traditionally produced a graduate who learned "how to (do tasks) almost to perfection"[20]. These programs tend to produce graduates who take pride in efficiently "performing assigned routine tasks" and making decisions on the basis of established policy, but who are not well prepared "to engage confidently in problem solving and decision making"[21]. Diploma graduates constitute the largest percentage of nurses in hospitals. In many hospitals, nurses without exposure to any additional education move up the hierarchical ladder, accompanied by their nursing philosophy. Some of nursing's lack of autonomy in setting nursing standards in hospitals may be a direct consequence of this fact. Another outcome may be the staff nurse's reliance on departmentally oriented and controlled quality assurance programs as an unquestioned basis for nursing standards.

If educational preparation is a primary force in setting standards, then graduates of diploma schools would be more likely to equate quality with efficiency in task performance and adherence to rules, either written or informally sanctioned by authority figures such as doctors, administrators, and nursing supervisors. Independent nursing standards might well be neglected, since the standards do not derive from "acceptable" sources.

A second type of educational preparation is the associate degree program, a two-year program designed to prepare nurse technicians who are equipped with beginning nursing skills and able to carry out selected nursing functions. The new graduate of this program is not an expert technician but rather a neophyte in need of much guidance and supervised practice before assuming a full technical nursing role. The efforts of faculty to increase theory in these programs has resulted in little more than a "duplication of the baccalaureate curriculum but only in a watered down form"[22]. This limited theoretical base prevents graduates of associate degree programs from performing effectively in independent problem-solving and decision-making roles. Their education was not designed to prepare them for the professional role. There has been a steady rise in the number of graduates of these programs. For example, in New York State in 1973–1974, 47.1 percent of nurses graduating from registered nurse programs were from associate degree programs[23]. Rotkovich believes that this nurse is poorly prepared, because she lacks the "scientific and theoretical base necessary to make nursing diagnoses, plan and implement care, evaluate the effect of her intervention and record her actions in a form that indicates that a reflective, intellectual process has taken place"[24]. The process just described is essential to the setting of independent nursing standards. In agencies where little or no guidance is provided, graduates of associate degree programs are unlikely to set independent standards for nursing care. Under some conditions, where their knowledge base is taxed beyond its limits, they may set unsafe standards.

Producing the smallest number of graduates is the baccalaureate program. Graduates of baccalaureate programs are presumed to have acquired the ability to do effective problem solving and decision making, exactly the abilities that are needed for independent standard setting. However, baccalaureate graduates enter practice with limited expertise in the procedures and functions required by agencies and are often quite unrealistic in their expectations about standards of care. The baccalaureate graduate faced with conflict between bureaucratic values and the professional values engendered by her education has three choices, according to Johnson: "she may accommodate to the system, leave the system, or live in the system with a high degree of dissatisfaction"[25]. In relation to hospitals, leaving the system has been the popular choice. Baccalaureate nurses who remain in the hospital either accommodate, accepting the standards of the predominant nursing group, or do not internalize the standards, although they perform at the expected level.

Educational preparation is not the sole influence on the standards set by the individual practitioner. Additional learning experiences, either as an outcome of practice or through formal continuing education, can change the nurse's values, skills, and decision-making abilities. Despite teachers' exhortations to continue learning after graduation, many nurses have tended to assume that the most important learning occurred in their basic education and that pursuit of additional education is not necessary. Today, most nurses express a need for continuing education, and many do participate in such programs; a steady number are moving from associate degree or diploma status to baccalaureate degree preparation. There may be a considerable difference in the standards set by the nurse who is pursuing postgraduate education and those set by a nurse who is not. The latter individual's standards may have crystallized at the level achieved at graduation.

Many nurses cite inservice education programs as not only valuable but the only source of postgraduate education. These programs can be very valuable, but for a professional nurse, they should be only one of a number of sources of education. Inservice programs are designed to meet agency goals and therefore the performance standards set by the department are the ones that serve as the goals for the inservice program. Increasingly, inservice departments are charged with offering only programs that can be justified in terms of training personnel to fulfill their assigned tasks and functions. This quite legitimate but narrow purpose limits the contribution of inservice programs to the professional nurse's growth. Further, for the nurse to set standards that are professionally sound, she needs to be exposed to many viewpoints, not just those of one agency.

What resources are available to the nurse seeking to keep up with changes in both nursing practice and in clinical knowledge and skills? Are there educational institutions offering programs both for academic advancement and/or continuing education? Is the nurse active in professional organizations and clinical specialty organizations that help keep her informed? If the nurse is not close to centers of learning and is unable to participate in organizational activities, what other resources, such as two-way radio programs and closed circuit television programs, are available? To what extent does the nurse participate in available activities? In today's rapidly changing world, access to accurate and current information is a major factor in determining the level of standards the nurse will set in practice.

The boy who stuck his finger in the dyke to stop the flood is a lonely and frightened figure. So, too, is the nurse who steps out of the crowd to attempt to bring about change in the standards of nursing care. There are very real and threatening sanctions that can be used by agencies, departments, groups, and individuals to bring this nurse into line. Unfortunately, the profession has failed to unite behind the venturesome nurse whose goals they approve of but will not support. This emphasizes the importance of peer support in standard setting. Respect for and from colleagues in the department and in the community stimulates the practitioner to be more aggressive in examining and resetting standards and initiating change in practice. Nolan believes that in order for nurses to control their own practice (and standard setting is an important aspect of control), they must, whatever their educational or experiential backgrounds and current positions, come together and consult with each other to solve nursing problems[26]. Access to a peer support system might encourage nurses to be more autonomous in standard setting.

A crucial factor in standard setting is the individual nurse's willingness to assume an autonomous role in practice. No one would argue that nursing has been and still is identified with women. The male-female, superordinate-subordinate roles of doctors and nurses is well known. In hospitals, the largest number of nurses are graduated from diploma programs. Mauksh describes the predominant personality characteristics of these graduates as being nonassertive, low in risk taking, and lacking in personal autonomy[27]. The second largest group of nurses in hospitals are associate degree graduates, whose education does not prepare them to exercise leadership in setting nursing standards. However, the individual attracted to an associate degree program may not demonstrate the same characteristics as the diploma graduate. The associate degree programs, usually conducted in community colleges, do not indoctrinate the nursing student into a subordinate role to the degree that hospital-operated diploma schools have done. This graduate, if not defeated by a system that rarely acknowledges the need for longer orientation and guided performance, may, after gaining confidence in her role, be more assertive about nursing practice. The question is whether this individual's educational preparation is equal to the task of a more assertive role.

Perhaps as important as personality characteristics are the individual's personal goals and her reasons for selecting nursing as an occupation. The nurse who chose nursing as a profession and views it as a lifelong occupation is likely to be concerned with standards for nursing care. Some individuals are attracted by the relatively low cost of nursing education in diploma schools or community colleges and believe that nursing offers an opportunity to climb the career ladder. Some of these individuals find nursing care distasteful. Many such nurses aim at achieving "status" positions as head nurse or supervisor to enhance their economic and social position. Their abilities to set nursing care standards are often limited.

Another type of practicing nurse whose standard setting abilities are open to question is what might be called the "second-car" or "pay-off-the-mortgage" nurse. This is usually a married nurse who works part time and whose goal is to contribute to the family budget to buy "extras." The husband is considered the primary wage earner and the wife's job is a "little" job to help buy the luxuries, to get her out of the house, or to provide a modicum of independence by earning her own money. Such goals tend to diminish the importance of her career to this practitioner and raise questions about the concern she would have for setting and maintaining nursing standards.

The list of influences that affect the nurse's standards in practice can be lengthened. For example, the individual whose original goal was medicine may well develop a high level of knowledge and competency in setting standards for components of nursing related to medical diagnoses and therapy while showing less concern for psycho-social problems. The latter area is not so highly valued by medicine. If nursing is to maintain its professional status, practitioners must examine their goals to assess their impact on their personal standards for nursing care.

SUMMARY AND CONCLUSIONS

In most hospitals, the staff nurse is viewed by administration as functioning at the lowest administrative level—the "boss on the job," so to speak. To this individual is assigned the actual "physical task of carrying out the organization's objectives"[28]. These tasks may not directly relate to nursing and, in point of fact, quite often do not. In carrying out these objectives, this individual is expected to adhere to the standards of and respond to the influence of the administrative, medical, and nursing hierarchy above her. Success of administrators in the several hierarchies is demonstrated by the degree of compliance of the staff nurse in meeting administrative standards and objectives.

At odds with the deferential behavior expected by administrators is the belief held by an increasing number of nurses that "control of nursing practice belongs in the hands of our own professionals," with its implications of autonomy in standard setting and practice[29]. Professional leaders and professional groups exert pressure on the staff nurse to seek autonomy in the practice setting. They imply that the practicing nurse should, after identifying what nursing practice is, move away from the role of "soldier on the line" in the administrative hierarchy and aim for a more professional staff role in the agency. The course followed by the nurse, who is being pressured in different directions by agency administrators and by nursing leaders, will be influenced by most of the factors discussed in this chapter. The final proof that autonomous nursing practice will result in a very high standard of nursing care advantageous to the public must still be demonstrated. It is obvious that nursing's lack of control over standard setting and practice in many agencies has led to a reduction in the quality of nursing care. Thus it seems reasonable to assume that the greater the autonomy permitted nursing in standard setting and practice, the higher the standards of nursing care will be. In Figures 2 through 4, we attempt to illustrate the relative impact of the various categories of factors on the achievement of a high standard of nursing care. This standard is based on the presumption that the client achieved the most desirable possible outcome as the result of goal-directed nursing intervention. In Figure 2, utopia is represented. The height of each of the steps represents positive factors in each category that provide support for autonomous, high-level nursing practice. The outcome is the achievement of a high standard of nursing care for the client.

In Figures 3 and 4, more potentially realistic combinations of factors are represented. The height of the blocks continues to represent the positive factors affecting the standards of nursing care. But in these figures, not all blocks are of equal height, to indicate that not all factors in each category support positive nursing standards.

In Figure 3, more support emanates from the patient, the department of nursing, and the nurse than from the other categories. A moderately high standard of care might be achieved with this combination of supportive factors. In Figure 4, on the other hand, the combination of positive factors might favor the development of high expectations of nursing care in society, in the prospective patient and, to a degree, in the agency, but the lack of strong support from allied health workers, the nursing department, and from the nurse herself could keep the standard of nursing care well below the desired standard. Nurses must be able to identify positive factors in society, the patient, and the agency and use these factors in improving standards of practice. Recognition of the existence of these factors and their impact should provide nurses with cues to the action they must take, either individually or collectively, to improve the quality of nursing care.

Factors Providing Positive Support for Nursing

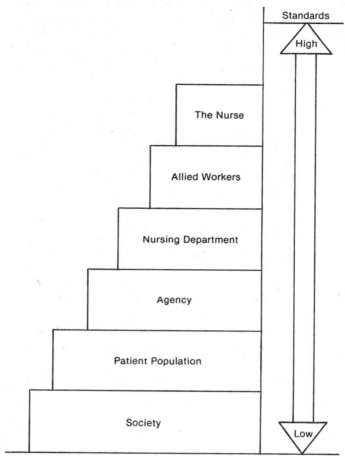

FIGURE 2.   RELATIONSHIP OF FACTORS TO LEVEL OF QUALITY OF NURS-
ING CARE—ALL FACTORS SUPPORTIVE OF NURSING

One way that nursing can improve its public image is to come to terms with its multiple levels of preparation and reduce the categories of nurse to manageable proportions. If professional autonomy requires that nurses have certain knowledge and skills primarily associated with baccalaureate education, then it seems logical that nursing do something about educational and licensure requirements. For this, nurses of all backgrounds must come together not only to hammer out what nursing is, but also to decide what level of education will be required of its practitioners.

If nursing hopes to be taken seriously as a health care profession, it must shed the image, held by some groups, of a social, economic, and even therapeutic haven for individuals unable to cope in any other milieu. Every effort should be made to attract and admit to nursing programs applicants capable of meeting the requirements of

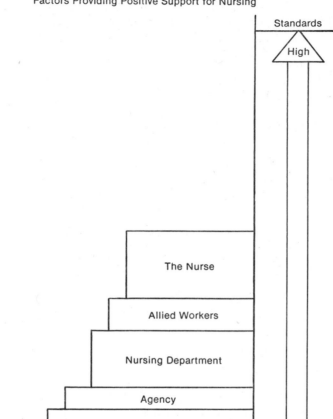

Factors Providing Positive Support for Nursing

FIGURE 3. RELATIONSHIP OF FACTORS TO LEVEL OF QUALITY OF NURS-
ING CARE—VARIATION IN DEGREE OF SUPPORT

the program. Nursing must convince secondary school counselors and others in education to halt the all-too-frequent practice of encouraging application to nursing schools for students who are considered inadequate for other fields of endeavor. It is the health needs of society that must be met, not the needs of the prospective practitioner of nursing.

Those involved in the maintenance, restoration, and repair of the human system are dealing with the most complex system on earth. Let us in nursing recognize this and set our standards accordingly. Even if educational programs for professional nurses have attracted adequately endowed applicants, other nursing personnel have frequently required inordinate amounts of supervision to ensure even safe care. It is now frequently assumed that nursing care is whatever this level of worker can provide. The recipients of such care might be grateful if professional

Factors Providing Positive Support for Nursing

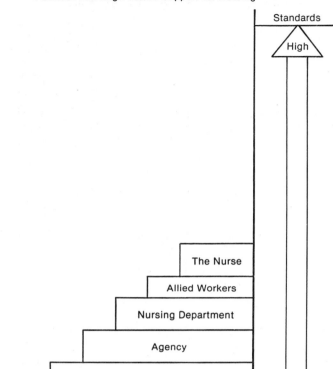

FIGURE 4.   RELATIONSHIP OF FACTORS TO LEVEL OF QUALITY OF NURS-
ING CARE—VARIATION IN DEGREE OF SUPPORT

nurses were more demanding about requirements not only for their own education, but also for that of auxilliary personnel. Our educational programs should focus on nursing, the requisite supportive social and physical sciences, and the development of problem-solving and decision-making skills. It seems desirable that the teachers of these programs become both practitioners and educators so that they do not "idealize how they should or would respond" to a patient's nursing problem, but are able to relate the ideal to reality[30]. There should be closer dialogue between nursing service and nursing educators in setting standards. Attempt to alter established attitudes and patterns of practice that militate against nursing autonomy calls for assertiveness and risk taking, which are not characteristic in the nursing community. Nurses are going to have to develop new patterns of behavior to achieve these ends. Nurse educators are not exempt from the need to change. As educators become more involved in practice, the risk-taking aspects of assertiveness become more obvious. It is their assertiveness as nurses, not as teachers that nursing students need as a role model.

Another area in which nursing must become more active is politics. The recent development of nursing political action groups indicates increasing sophistication about the sources and uses of political power. Political clout can help nursing obtain desirable, even essential, health legislation for the public, encourage support for nursing education, and influence regulatory legislation in the direction of desirable standards of nursing care.

In the last analysis, it is the individual nurse who determines the standards of nursing care that prevails. If these standards require a profession that is autonomous, then the nurse must develop the self-image of an autonomous professional practitioner and the skills and assertiveness necessary for the role.

REFERENCES

1. Kramer, M. *Reality Shock: Why Nurses Leave Nursing.* St. Louis: C.V. Mosby, 1974, p. 73.
2. Donabedian, A. Promoting quality through evaluating the process of patient care. *Med. Care,* Vol. 6, No. 3, 1968, p. 182.
3. Donabedian, A. 1968, p. 183.
4. American Nurses Association. *Guidelines for Peer Review.* Kansas City: American Nurses Association, 1973, p. 1.
5. Zimmer, M.J. "Quality Assurance for Nursing," in *Quality Assurance for Nursing Care.* Kansas City: American Nurses Association and American Hospital Association, 1973, p. 11.
6. Somers, A. *Health Care in Transition—Directions for the Future.* Chicago: Hospital Research and Educational Trust, 1971, p. 21.
7. Quinn, N. and Somers, A.R. The patient's Bill of Rights, a significant aspect of the consumer revolution. *Nurs. Outlook,* Vol. 22, No. 4, 1974, p. 240.
8. Annas, G.J. *The Rights of Hospitalized Patients. An American Civil Liberties Union Handbook.* New York: Avon Books, 1975, p. 6.
9. Ainsworth, T.J. "The American Hospital Association's Quality Control Program, American Medical Association's Peer Review Program, and the Social Security Amendments for Professional Standards Review Organizations," in *Quality Assurance for Nursing Care.* Kansas City: American Nurses Association and American Hospital Association, 1973, p. 63.
10. Mauksch, I. and David, M.L. Prescription for survival. *Am. J. Nurs.,* Vol. 72, No. 12, 1972, p. 2189.
11. Kelly, L.Y. Nursing practice acts. *Am. J. Nurs.,* Vol. 74, No. 7, 1974, p. 1310.
12. *New York State Education Law, Article 139, Section 6902.*
13. Donovan, H.M. *Nursing Service Administration: Managing The Enterprise.* St. Louis: C.V. Mosby, 1975, p. 4.
14. American Nurses Association. 1973, p. 1.
15. Zimmer, M.J. 1973, p. 9.
16. Ramphal, M. Peer review. *Am. J. Nurs.,* Vol. 74, No. 1, 1974, p. 66.
17. Davidson, G.E. Collaborating with nursing staff in developing standards of care. *Nurs. Clin. North Am.,* Vol. 8, No. 2, 1973, p. 220.
18. Rosasco, L.C. Of nursing practice and nursing practitioners. *Hospitals, JAHA,* Vol. 48, 1974, p. 107.
19. Rosasco, L.C. 1974, p. 108.
20. Rotkovitch, R. The AD nurse: a nursing service perspective. *Nurs. Outlook,* Vol. 24, No. 4, 1976, p. 234.
21. Nolan, M.G. Wanted: colleagueship in nursing. *J. Nurs. Admin.,* Vol. 6, No. 3, 1976, p. 41.
22. Rotkovitch, R. 1976, p. 235.
23. *Educational Preparation for Practical and Professional Nursing, 1974.* Albany: SUNY, State Education Department, Office of Professional Education, 1975, p. 11.
24. Rotkovitch, R. 1976, p. 235.
25. Johnson, N.D. The profession-bureaucratic conflict. *J. Nurs. Admin.,* Vol. 1, No. 1, 1971, p. 34.
26. Nolan, M.G. 1976, p. 43.
27. Mauksch, H.O. "Nursing: Churning for Change," in *Handbook of Medical Sociology,* H.E. Freeman (ed.). Englewood Cliffs, N.J.: Prentice-Hall, 1972, p. 216.
28. Simon, H. *Administrative Behavior,* (2nd ed.). New York: Macmillan, 1957, p. 2.
29. Nolan, M.G. 1976, p. 43.
30. Kramer, M. 1974, p. 60.

Chapter 7

Philosophy, Purpose, and Objectives: Why Do We Have Them?

Marjorie Moore Cantor

Most nursing departments can produce documents entitled, "Philosophy, Purpose, and Objectives," designed either for the department or for special units, divisions, or programs. They usually are carefully prepared by conscientious nurses. But if examined ·closely, these statements frequently have no referents in the activities for which they are to provide guidance. In other words, many of these statements are written as a task which one does because it is there, and these statements have no function other than to be viewed by accreditors and other distinguished visitors.

Because of some undefined, uneasy feeling about the task, it is not uncommon for nurses developing such documents to seek help from "authorities," from whom they are likely to receive advice on *how* these statements should be written and *what* they should contain. Seldom are they told *why* these statements are written or *what one does with them* after they have been completed. For this reason, the writers of such statements tend to focus on the task of developing the wording rather than the ideas, and the statements are seldom thought of as a

base for planning and implementing the operations with which the documents are supposedly concerned.

Because of this focus on the writing, the documents tend to include concepts phrased in professional jargon, which have been accepted uncritically. The statements achieve social approval within the group, but they are difficult to translate into action. Concern with "man as a unique entity interacting with his environment," "providing the patient with individualized care," "the democratic process as a basis for administration," or similar thoughts are frequently encountered within these papers. To the individuals who expound them, such ideas can provide satisfaction at only a verbal level because any attempts at implementation reveal that they are not clearly conceptualized by the individuals proposing them. This tendency to make use of pot-boiler statements culled from the folklore of nursing does serve a purpose of sorts: it protects nurses from looking at the realities of their jobs and evaluating their own activities. If the philoso-

Reprinted with permission from *The Journal of Nursing Administration*, Volume 1, Number 3, May-June, 1971, pp. 9–14. © 1971.

phy, purpose and objectives are stated in sufficiently nonfunctional terms, the ideas in question cannot be used as a basis for checking whether activities are in line with what one *says* she believes and is trying to achieve. This avoidance of self-examination is not restricted to nurses; we share it with the rest of humanity.

Why bother with statements of philosophy, purpose, and objectives if they are seldom functional? Would the time be better spent in developing the operation itself? The answer to the latter question is *yes*, if such statements are developed as an end rather than as a beginning. *However, they can be very useful if they are developed to be functional,* if the philosophy, purpose, and objectives are developed as statements from which the operation of the unit, service, or program takes its direction. It is helpful to look at the development of philosophy, purpose, and objectives from the standpoint of how they can provide guidance in the operation for which they were written.

The statement of *purpose* describes the reason for being—the why of the operation. A clear understanding of purpose by all involved is primary to the total operation. The statement of *philosophy* as it is used in this context is an explanation of the system of beliefs that determines the way one achieves the purpose. The *objectives* are statements of the criteria by which one measures the degree to which the purpose is achieved.

PURPOSE

Clarification of purpose, then, has first priority for the development of any operation. For any nursing agency or program the ultimate purpose is to provide quality nursing care to patients. But a nursing department may be established to accomplish different aspects of this purpose, and

programs within the department will have various goals that contribute to the major purpose. It is important, for example, that a nursing department within a teaching and research hospital recognize that the nursing department was established to provide a nursing environment which supports and encourages research and teaching. To provide such an environment, the research and teaching function must be reconciled with the ultimate goal of all nursing—the provision of quality nursing care to patients. The reconciliation of these two purposes determines the kind of operation to be established.

Any nursing department must determine how the purposes of nursing relate to the purpose for which the establishment was formed. Furthermore, when a program is developed *within* a nursing department, a realistic appraisal of its contribution to the overall purpose of quality nursing care is necessary. If the expected contribution is not stated in realistic terms, is not clearly understood, and is not used as a basis for planning, it is probable that the program initiated will be ineffective in the achievement of excellence in nursing care.

The inservice education programs of many nursing services demonstrate what is likely to happen. The purpose of an inservice education program is to educate the staff to the requirements of the job and to improve the quality of work they do. But time after time programs are selected for their interest value only, and they are evaluated in terms of the nurses' *pleasure* in the program. If the purpose of a program is to build morale, then providing programs that make the staff feel contented achieves the purpose. But if the purpose is to teach staff to perform in a way that realizes benefits to *patients*, it is likely that such an approach would garner minimal benefits in improved function.

If one is establishing a unit for the care of ambulatory patients who are either in the process of diagnosis or preparation for returning home, it is important to determine first whether the purpose is to reduce the cost of care to the patient and the hospital, or whether it is to help patients adjust to and cope with changes related to their illness. It would make a difference in the kind of staff required. It is customary in many hospitals to think of this type of unit as a minimal care unit and, if one defines minimal care as reduced services and care provided by non-professional personnel, one could achieve the purpose of reduced cost to the hospital and patient. However, the second purpose cannot be achieved in this way. This is not to say that one purpose is superior to the other—only that knowledge and clarification of purpose are necessary for effective operation.

Almost any operation can benefit from a careful examination of its purpose and the extent to which the procedure involved is related to that purpose. Even the establishment of a policy becomes more meaningful when the purpose is thoughtfully determined. Examination of policies and practices long adhered to in nursing departments will frequently reveal that, although the policy is supported vigorously, the reason for it has long been forgotten or no longer exists.

PHILOSOPHY

A philosophy for an institution, department, committee or program is a statement of the system of beliefs which direct the individuals in a particular group in the achievement of their purpose. It should be a statement that can be referred to as an explanation of why things are carried out in the way they are.

A collective philosophy covers those things about which the group is collectively concerned and on which decisions are required. Nurses involved in the preparation of a statement of philosophy about their nursing department may have been encouraged to develop first a statement about Man, then one about nursing generally, and then one about the department. This is a pretentious approach and one that has little usefulness in helping to establish desirable practices within the department. A nursing department does not operate as a group with respect to issues on Man, his concerns about his identity, his relations to society, or his habit patterns. The concerns of the nursing department are the patient who comes to the institution for nursing care and the nursing care that is provided for him. The more a statement of philosophy restricts itself to the actual collective concerns and a clear expression of them, the more meaningful will that statement be.

A statement of philosophy can be useful only if it serves as a directive to those involved regarding the way the purpose is to be achieved. It should state clearly the premises which govern the operation. If one cannot look to the philosophy for this kind of direction, then it, too, becomes no more than an exercise in the manipulation of words and phrases.

Many philosophies deal with socially accepted ideas such as the "democratic ideal" and the "rights of the human being as an individual." Yet if nurses would ask themselves how the nursing department manifests this belief in a democratic system, they would be hard put to come up with an answer. If, in contrast, the nursing department asserts that it believes each patient should be treated in relation to his nursing needs rather than his economic situation or other social factors, one can show that this belief has been implemented because, in fact, the indigent patient is provided with nursing care equal to that received by the wealthiest patient, and the delinquent is cared for as assiduously as the pillar of the church. This kind of conformity of action to belief can be continually examined for the extent to which it is being observed by members of the nursing staff. A statement to the effect that one believes in the democratic process or that one believes in the inherent dignity of man is too ill-defined to have meaning and to serve as a basis for determining how one might operate. If a department cannot say that this is what we do or expect of our members in order to conform to our beliefs, the philosophy is simply a group of words set down to meet some need of those writing them. It will have little to do with the department's actual operation.

There are many values and beliefs to be examined when considering the operation of a nursing department within a hospital. How do the department's members feel about the skill level required for a minimal care as opposed to a special care unit? What do they believe about the difference in nursing care requirements for different kinds of nursing units? Are they planning to have specialists function in special care units and less prepared individuals in general or minimal care units? What do they believe about the role of educational programs in the department? Should the people responsible for developing the programs be the same individuals who provide the direct care? If not, should the former be at least as competent as the latter?

A philosophy about a nursing department or a program within the department that simply reiterates the accepted generalities of the day might better not be written at all because it not only fails to serve as a basis for clarifying the values of the group, but it also requires time and energy to prepare. Even without thoughtful expression of group values, time can be wasted on the sheer mechanics of writing and the creation of literary effect.

OBJECTIVES

If an objective is to be useful, it must be stated in terms of the results to be achieved so that it can be used as a basis for assessing the effectiveness of the process carried out. To be sure that whatever objectives are chosen can serve this purpose, one must consider them in terms of the purpose and philosophy of the operation.

For example, a nursing care objective for a hospital nursing department might state, "arrangements will be made or patient will be prepared for continuation of necessary regimen of posthospitalization care." An objective stated in this way indicates the group believes that nursing responsibility should extend beyond the confines of the hospital and that they intend to assess the achievement of this purpose by observing results with patients.

In contrast, as an objective, "Public Health referrals are sent as needed," indicates a focus on process rather than on results. If the objectives are written in terms of the method to be used rather than the results to be gained, there is greater danger that certain nursing interventions will continue to be implemented whether they are effective or not. Objectives for most projects are written in terms of the process rather than results. Some familiar examples: Patients will be taught about their illness. Patients will receive nursing care appropriate to the stages of their illness. The patient will be treated as an individual and his care modified according to his needs.

Although in each case the patient is mentioned, the focus tends to be on the activities of the nurse rather than on what the patient will manifest to indicate that the process *was appropriate*. Because nurses do tend to concentrate on the activities of nursing rather than on the effects to be achieved, it is necessary to emphasize the difference. The distinction may seem to be unimportant, but it must be kept in mind if objectives are to be written with thought given to why they are written and how they are to be used. If one is to use objectives as criteria for assessing the extent to which purposes have been achieved, then it is important to structure the objectives to indicate *what must be observed in the patient* to show that the nursing care in question was appropriate.

For purposes of explicitness, the general objectives that are written for the whole department must be defined in more specific terms to apply to particular groups of patients. In the case of the posthospital regimen objective, specification of posthospital regimen for newborn babies might include such items as the mother's demonstrating that she can bathe and feed the baby and that she understands and uses information about particular situations in infant care. For a group of patients who have had radical mastectomies, concern may be focused on the ability to perform required exercises and the ability to identify symptoms that they must look for and what they should do if those symptoms exist. Or the interest might be in a family's ability to provide care when a patient cannot or will not assume responsibility for his own care.

When evaluating the achievement of these objectives, one should not ask "Was the mother taught?" More appropriate questions are "What does the mother know and what can she do?" Instead of "Did someone teach the exercises to the patient?" ask "Can the patient do the exercises and will she be likely to do them?"

Of course, the most meaningful evaluation would come from direct observation of the patient outside of the hospital. To the extent that one could have access to such information, she could revise the objective to "carries out regimen of care prescribed." But few hospital nursing departments have access to this kind of information, and since objectives need to be stated in terms of evidence that can be evaluated *directly*, this particular goal may have to be formulated with a focus on determining what behavior can be observed *now* (prior to leaving the hospital) that is most likely to lead to desired *future* behavior.

Most of the other objectives of a nursing department can be evaluated directly. For example, nursing departments will want to see that patients do not develop such complications as postoperative pneumonia, contractures, decubiti, and infections. In the case of postoperative pneumonia, for example, what one would look for in the patient to determine that he was free of pneumonia would need to be described. This description, which might include "full, easy respirations involving excursion of the chest, rate of breathing within normal limits, and body temperature normal," would serve as the definition for "freedom from postoperative pneumonia." The patient might have been "turned, coughed, and deep breathed" as a means of achieving the goal, but the evaluation criteria of the effectiveness of nursing care, or in other words, the objectives, would be in terms of the description of the patient's condition, not the method used. If one accepts results as manifested in the patient's condition as the only criteria for quality care, then one can be sure that nursing measures will be more critically examined for their effectiveness in achieving their purpose.

In the case of programs that contribute to the total purpose, the principle is the same—to evaluate the effectiveness, one must identify the objectives in terms of what is to be accomplished.

The staff development, or inservice education program, can again be used as a point of illustration. One would assume that the purpose of the staff educational program is to prepare staff members to be able to achieve the nursing care objectives. The program would presumably include a variety of activities. Of recent concern has been the training of individuals to meet the emergency care requirement for patients experiencing cardiac arrest. If one of the objectives of the inservice education program is to "provide training in the cardio-pulmonary resuscitation procedure," then the presentation of the training materials will satisfy that goal. If, on the other hand, the objective is to prepare staff so that "patients receive immediate care in emergency situations (cardiac arrest)" then the educational program takes on an entirely different dimension. To make sure that individuals continue to perform adequately requires time for planned practice, review, and frequent evaluation with use of predetermined evaluation criteria. Educating a staff member to carry out procedures evaluated in terms of results with patients is quite a different matter from presenting programs and training materials—different in the material to be presented and techniques of teaching.

As is true of statements of purpose and philosophy, statements of objectives call for thoughtful examination of the reason for which they are being developed. If objectives are presented in terms of results to be achieved and defined in terms of what can be observed, they can serve as useful tools for evaluation of nursing care and personnel performance, and as a basis for planning educational programs, staffing, requisition of supplies and equipment, and other functions associated with the nursing department. If they are not written in such terms, they may serve only to obscure actual departmental purposes.

Nurses embarking on the development of statements of purpose, philosophy, and objectives as described here, will find that it is easier to state ideas in vague generalities than to state them in terms that can be measured in the reality of everyday activities. But this more difficult task of stating what we want to accomplish in measurable terms is essential to the provision of a service that is beneficial to patients. Thoughtfully prepared statements of purpose, philosophy, and objectives based on reality, understood and used by those responsible for implementation, can promote efficiency and effectiveness in the operation of institutions, departments, and programs. Statements lacking these qualities are merely collections of words.

Chapter 8

The Patient's Bill of Rights and the Nurse

M. Elizabeth Carnegie

In 1973, the American Hospital Association issued a statement, "A Patient's Bill of Rights," with the expectation that observance of these rights would contribute to more effective patient care. Condensed, the statement affirms that the patient has the right to:

1. considerate and respectful care;
2. complete current information from his doctor about diagnosis, treatment, and prognosis in terms he can understand, and the name of the doctor handling his case;
3. information from his doctor that enables him to give informed consent before any procedure or treatment starts, and the name of the person administering it;
4. refuse treatment to the extent the law allows, and know the medical consequences of doing so;
5. privacy in his medical care program that includes discreet conduct of examination and treatment, confidentiality in discussion of his case, and his permission for anyone not directly involved in his care to be present at case discussion, consultation, examination, and treatment;
6. have communications and records concerning his case kept confidential;
7. reasonable response to request for services, within the hospital's capacity, as indicated by the urgency of his case; complete information as to the reasons for transfer to another institution if necessary (including the alternatives to such transfer), and the knowledge that the other institution has accepted him for transfer;
8. information about any relationship between his hospital and other health-care or educational institutions, as far as it concerns his case, and about any professional relationships among individuals (by name) who are treating him;
9. know if the hospital proposes to conduct human experimentation affecting his case or treatment, and to refuse to participate in such research projects;
10. expect reasonable continuity of care (including knowledge of what appointment times and doctors are available, and where), and to have the hospital provide for his doctor's (or a delegate's) letting him know what his continuing health-care requirements will be after discharge;
11. examine his bill and have it explained to him, regardless of who pays it; and
12. know what hospital rules and regulations apply to his conduct while he is a patient[1].

Reprinted with permission from *Nursing Clinics of North America*, Volume 9, Number 3, September, 1974, pp. 557-562.

Since the issuance of the AHA statement, patients' rights have been explored separately by such groups as hospital administrators, nurses, and lawyers.

Hospital Administrators

The first patients' rights workshop ever conducted in a hospital in New York was sponsored last year by the National Association of Health Services Executives, which is an all-Black group, and the Kings County Hospital Center in Brooklyn. The purposes of the workshop, which was more like a forum, were: (1) to make the community aware of the services available at the hospital; (2) to provide the community with the opportunity to express any opinion or complain about any aspect of the hospital; and (3) to advise the patient of his rights. One of the concerns expressed by the community participants was in the area of research. They questioned research because of their belief that minority groups, particularly in municipal hospitals, are victims of experimentation. Another vital point was made: "Informing patients of their rights is only a halfway measure. All hospital personnel must become informed of these rights and make an effort to see that they are enforced"[2].

Nurses

Many state nurses' associations have endorsed the AHA statement and have passed resolutions on patients' rights. The resolution passed by the Texas Nurses Association last year, "supports the position that every person accepted for health care services must be provided safe and continual care. In addition, persons seeking health care services are entitled to the right to make decisions about the care they will accept." The resolution also stated that providers of care must inform their community if there exist limitations for safe and continual care[3].

Lawyers

In recent years the legal profession has begun to recognize that some powerless groups need their rights protected. At a seminar for lawyers in New York in December, 1973, the 500 participants discussed recent court rulings in several states regarding the rights of patients in mental institutions. One was a decision made by a three-judge Federal court in Wisconsin to the effect that a person cannot be committed to a mental hospital unless he is informed that conversations with a state psychiatrist could be used against him. Another was a ruling in Michigan made by a Federal court that corrective brain surgery on a violent criminal could in part violate his First Amendment "freedom to generate ideas"[4].

This article will focus mainly on the item in the American Hospital Association statement that deals with *research*, because many of the other items may be considered "threads" that run through the whole research process, for example, informed consent, considerate and respectful care, privacy, confidentiality, and the right to refuse to participate in human experimentation.

NURSE INVOLVEMENT

The ideas expounded in the AHA Bill of Rights are not new to nurses. Nurses all over the world are agreed on a code of ethics which states that "Inherent in nursing is respect for life, dignity, and rights of man. It is unrestricted by consideration of nationality, race, creed, color, age, sex, politics or social status"[5].

As nurses have participated in research, either directly or indirectly, they have adhered to these beliefs in protecting the rights of patients. With the accelerated growth of research, considerable concern has developed regarding a person's right to determine the extent to which he wishes to be studied—if at all. Nurses, who have been the subjects of much research, especially by social scientists, know the importance of consent and confidentiality and so can appreciate the ethics involved in research conducted on other human subjects. As someone so aptly put it, research without consent is espionage.

All professional associations, including the American Nurses' Association, set standards of ethics to protect the rights and welfare of human subjects in the research process. However, the news media have brought to the attention of the American public examples of experiments that are being performed on human subjects by professionals in training and demonstration projects which violate these rights. One of these projects, sponsored by the Federal government, is the Tuskegee (Alabama) syphilis experiment. Survivors informed about their plight have filed a suit in the Alabama Federal court. In this experiment, begun 40 years ago, 399 victims of the disease were left untreated and uninformed of the nature of their illness. The victims, all Black and all men, were told they were joining a health program. The purpose of the study was to determine the long-term effects of syphilis on untreated victims. All of the participants, 85 percent of whom had less than a sixth grade education, were persuaded to join a social club named after the public health nurse who supervised the study in the field[6].

The above is just one example of how patients' rights are flagrantly violated, and nurses, knowingly or unknowingly, can become involved in this violation. Others under investigation include involuntary sterilization at a federally funded birth control clinic in Montgomery, Alabama[7]; compulsory sterilization in North Carolina[8]; and involvement of children in experimental hepatitis programs at a New York State school for the mentally retarded as a prerequisite for admission[9].

Because of seemingly unethical practices regarding informed consent, privacy, undue risks, and inducements, the Federal government, pressured by consumer groups, has created a set of guidelines pertaining to the protection of human subjects[10].

As the layman has become more and more aware of his human rights, more demands are being made on the Federal government to guarantee compliance by those engaged in human experimentation. Hopefully, nurses will not only observe ethical principles when participating in research, but will have the courage to refuse to become a part of unethical investigations, keeping in mind the American Nurses' Association's guidelines for the nurse researcher in clinical research. The guidelines stress the protection of human rights in research: (1) the right to privacy; (2) the right to self-determination; (3) the right to conservation of personal resources; (4) the right to freedom from arbitrary hurt; and (5) the right to freedom from intrinsic risk of injury[11].

Nursing Research magazine has a policy that requires the nature of consent to be indicated in articles reporting research involving human subjects. The following is incorporated in its "Specifications for Manuscripts: A Guide for Prospective Authors": *"Nursing Research* is concerned that the rights and dignity of human subjects be considered in research. Therefore, one criterion for selection [of articles to be published] is evidence that the rights of individuals have been protected in the research reported." The investigator is expected to describe the safeguards used to insure privacy and answer such questions as: "What procedure was used to secure the consent of the subjects? How fully were the research and the procedures to be used explained to subjects; if some aspects could not be explained, how were these handled? How were data handled to ensure anonymity and confidentiality? Any explanation should enable a reader to determine how adequately the rights of individuals in each particular situation were protected[12].

NURSING'S BILL OF RIGHTS

The AHA statement does not make specific reference to the nurse. Nor were nurses involved in developing it. However, long before the American Hospital Association came forth with its statement, the National League for Nursing formulated and issued in 1959 a "Patient's Bill of Rights," which has culminated in a statement titled, "What People Can Expect of Modern Nursing Service"[13]. The NLN statement recognizes that nursing is an integral part of all health care and implies that rights involve responsibilities, and good nursing requires cooperation between the consumer and the provider of care.

The statement includes three basic assumptions: (1) Nursing care encompasses health promotion, the care and prevention of disease or disability, and rehabilitation, and involves teaching, counseling, and emotional support as well as the care of illness. (2) Nursing care is an integral part of total health care and is planned and administered in combination with related medical, educational, and welfare services. (3) Nursing personnel respect the individuality, dignity, and rights of every person, regardless of race, color, creed, national origin, or social or economic status.

Specifically, the bill states that the patient has a right to expect:

1. That he will receive the nursing care necessary to help him regain or maintain his maximum degree of health.

2. That the nursing personnel who care for him are qualified, through education, experience, and personality, to carry out the services for which they are responsible.

3. That the nursing personnel caring for him will be sensitive to his feelings and responsive to his needs.

4. That within the limits determined by his doctor, the patient and his family will be taught about his illness so that the patient can help himself, and his family can understand and help him.

5. That plans will be made with him and his family, or if necessary for him, so that if possible, continuing nursing and other necessary services will be available to him throughout the period of his need. These plans will involve the use of all appropriate personal and community resources.

6. That nursing personnel will assist in keeping adequate records and reports and will treat with confidence all personal matters that relate to the patient.

7. That efforts will be made by nursing personnel to adjust the surroundings of the patient so as to help him maintain or recover his health[14].

One of the strongest forces in the world today is the respect for the worth and dignity of every human being. This is the core of human rights. "Each person is an individual member of society who has rights, privileges and immunities which should be respected, regardless of race, creed, social or economic status, and has personal fears and needs which usually are exaggerated when there is a threat to his well-being"[15].

SUMMARY

Although some groups have objected to the AHA Patient's Bill of Rights and have written their own, in general the statement seems to be well accepted, especially by patients and nurses. It is hoped that the bill will help to foster better patient care for all.

Concern for the protection of human rights in the conduct of research seems to have gained national momentum through the help of the mass media. Nurses should pride themselves on a history of observing ethical standards in the conduct of research. In addition, nurses, although not involved in the development of the AHA statement, are proud of the fact that nurses, working with students, people in other disciplines, and the lay public, came out with a patient's bill of rights as early as 1959. This bill has culminated in a statement published by the National League for Nursing titled, "What People Can Expect of Modern Nursing Service."

Nurses have always known that the patient is the chief consideration. As Goodnow said in the very early part of the century, *"The patient is the main thing*...the reason for it all...the unit...the one chief consideration, the one whose welfare all else must be subordinated"[16].

Yes, patients' rights have always come first with nurses.

REFERENCES

1. American Hospital Association: A Patient's Bill of Rights. Chicago: *American Hospital Association*, 1972.
2. Lee, A.L. and Jacobs, G. Community relations workshop airs patient's rights. *Hospitals*, Vol. 47, Feb. 16, 1973, pp. 39–43.
3. Cornell, S. Nurses' patients' rights explored. *Texas Nursing*, Vol. 47, Oct. 1973, p. 1.
4. Seminar studies patients' rights. *New York Times*, Dec. 9, 1973.
5. International Council of Nurses: Code of Nurses—Ethical Concepts Applied to Nursing. *Intern. Nurs. Rev.*, Vol. 20, Nov.-Dec. 1973, p. 166.
6. Pollard, C. Black victims of syphilis experiment file class action suit for $1.8 billion. *Equal Justice*, Vol. 3, Autumn 1973, p. 2.
7. Keemer, E.B. Involuntary sterilization. *J. Nat. Med. Assoc.*, Vol. 65, Sept. 1973, p. 458.
8. Most important issue for immediate action. *Delta Newsletter*, Sept.-Oct. 1973, p. 2.
9. Marker, G. and Friedman, P.R. Rethinking Children's rights. *Children Today*, Vol. 2, Nov.-Dec. 1973, pp. 8–11.
10. Institutional Guide to DHEW Policy on Protection of Human Subjects. DHEW Publications No. (NIH), Vol. 72, Dec. 1, 1971, p. 102.
11. American Nurses' Association: The nurse in research: ANA guidelines on ethical values. *Nurs. Research,* Vol. 17, Mar.-Apr. 1968, pp. 104–107.
12. Notter, L.E. Protecting the rights of research subjects: An editorial. *Nurs. Research*, Vol. 18, Nov.-Dec. 1969, p. 483.
13. National League for Nursing: What People Can Expect of Modern Nursing Service. New York: *National League for Nursing*, 1959.
14. National League for Nursing, 1959.
15. Fuerst, E.V. and Wolff, L. *Fundamentals of Nursing*. 4th ed. Philadelphia: J.B. Lippincott Co., 1969, p. 32.
16. Goodnow, M. *First-Year Nursing*. 3rd ed. Philadelphia: W.B. Saunders Co., 1921, p. 19.

Chapter 9

Guidelines for Development of Outcome Criteria

Marie J. Zimmer and Associates

Appraisal or assessment of the outcomes of care, that is, alterations in patient health/wellness states, is a powerful means for quality assurance. It represents appraisal of the results of the collective effort of the peer group by the nurse peers involved together in the delivery of care to a specific patient population. When a nurse peer group's comparison of a set of health/wellness outcome criteria with the results of the care delivered demonstrates that actual outcomes are below the criteria level, selection and quality of activities are assessed to locate the cause. If the cause cannot be located and corrected through analysis and change in activities or resources that affect activities, solution should be sought through research.

Assessment of outcomes of nursing care, using a set of criteria specific to a particular patient population, is one cycle of a bi-cycle concept[1]. The data from the assessment of outcomes and subsequent analyses of activities are used as a basis for continuing education or other system changes. This is a second part of the cycle. The results of continuing education or system changes are determined in subsequent assessments in which the same set of criteria is applied. This reestablishes the two-part cycle.

When a set of outcome criteria is reapplied periodically to appraisal of the health/wellness outcomes of care for the specific patient population, the reappraisal shows trends in the quality of nursing care. It demonstrates whether the quality remains constant, improves, or regresses. The purpose of health/wellness outcome assessment is control and accounting for quality through monitoring and improvement.

To implement these beliefs about review of outcomes for nursing quality assurance, registered nurse peer groups or panels need to develop sets of patient health/wellness criteria, compare results of delivered care with criteria outcomes, and take action on the findings. The following set of guidelines is for the purpose of enabling peer groups to initiate and conduct their work. It is a summary of some of the assumptions and methods used by nurses who contributed to this symposium and their colleagues.

Reprinted with permission from *Nursing Clinics of North America*, Volume 9, Number 2, June, 1974, pp. 317–321.

CHARACTERISTICS OF PATIENT HEALTH/WELLNESS OUTCOME CRITERIA

1. A criterion is a standard or model that can be used in judging.
2. A criterion for assessment of the quality of nursing care must be relevant to the selected frame of reference, for example, outcome, activities, or resources.
3. Criteria stated in terms of outcomes, that is, alterations in the health status of the patients, are the frame of reference that is used when the person, peer group, or institution wishes to determine the result or benefit to the patients.
4. An outcome criterion always relates to the established objective.
5. A criterion that is relevant to results of nursing practice always relates to an outcome that is subject to change by one or more activities carried out by the nursing staff.
6. The outcome stated in a criterion must be possible to achieve.
7. Each criterion should be a statement of one specific outcome.
8. Each criterion should be written as specifically and concretely as possible.
9. A criterion must be appraisable. However, ease of assessment should not be used as a basis for accepting or rejecting a potential criterion. If a criterion is important, some assessment can be obtained.
10. Data that will be used to assess the degree to which a criterion is met should be observable.
11. A criterion should be stated to yield a range of scores or values. One way to achieve a range is to provide scales that depict time sequence, physiological and behavioral change, or recognized classifications.
12. A criterion should be phrased in positive terms, that is, presence of a quality or attribute, rather than negative terms, that is, absence of the quality.
13. A criterion should be tested to determine if it is understood and accepted by the registered nurses working with the specific patient population and consequently using the criterion.
14. A criterion should be tested to determine feasibility and applicability to the specific patient population.

FORMULATION OF SETS OF CRITERIA

15. Criteria should be written for a population of patients with commonalities that can be identified. A number of frameworks may be used to classify populations: for example, disease entities (myocardial infarction); developmental (adolescent); conceptual (rehabilitation); or syndrome (pain).
16. In initial work, populations should be selected that are common in the health care institution / agency / organization and create a significant volume of the patients who receive care and treatment.
17. Population characteristics that will cause variation in needs and outcomes for care should be used to subdivide the population so there is strong likelihood of comparability.
18. In selecting from among the total possible number of outcome criteria that could be developed for a particular patient population, priority should be given to the outcomes that make the most difference in the total result.
19. Criteria should be pertinent to the usual needs of the population under consideration. For example, for the ambulatory eye patient receiving photocoagu-

lation, skin care is important but usually not a critical care factor. Hence, a criterion would not be written for skin care.

20. Each criterion should be free from bias. Each patient to whom a criterion is applied should have an equal opportunity to obtain a good score. For example, skin condition for an aged patient and a youth might require different scales.

21. A set of criteria applicable to a specific patient population should include criteria for outcomes of care for members of the family or significant others.

22. Sets of criteria may be organized into sections using classifications relevant to type of outcome, for example, learning, physiological equilibrium, or social relationships.

23. Sets of criteria may be organized into sections using classifications relevant to stages of illness, for example, prevention, crisis, pre-convalescent and convalescent, restorative, and health maintenance. Nationally recognized classifications might also be used.

APPLICATION OF SETS OF CRITERIA TO ASSESSMENT OF DELIVERED CARE

24. Nursing audit is the usual method for comparing results of actual performance with the outcome criteria applicable to the specific patient population.

25. Patients' records are the usual source of data for results or benefits of delivered care.

26. Deductions about appropriate utilization of hospital, clinic, office, home care, nursing home, and other facilities can be made from criterion measures. From a set of criteria, judgments can be made about the point in a scale of progress at which the patient is ready for another setting for health care.

PEER GROUP, INTERDISCIPLINARY TEAM, AND CONSUMER PARTICIPATION IN ESTABLISHING OUTCOME CRITERIA

27. Criteria for assessing the quality of the outcomes of nursing practices are written, periodically reviewed, and updated by the institution's registered nurses who are expert in care of the specific patient population. These nurses evaluate and use criteria developed regionally and nationally to refine local criteria.

28. Registered nurse peer groups secure input from the patient so that the criteria include consumer needs and expectations. Consumers also provide data about results for use in comparisons of actual health results with criteria outcomes.

29. Development and application of sets of outcomes of health team care is desirable. In health review, there should be representation of all disciplines (nursing, medicine, allied health professions) who are accountable for a part of health care.

It should be kept in mind that nurses who are expert in care of very specific patient populations *know* the patient health/wellness results for which they are aiming and the observable evidence of patients' progress toward these outcomes. They either know or they have the communication skills and the trust needed to learn patients' expectations. The purpose of the preceding guidelines is to make it easier for these expert nurses to organize this knowledge into the form of criterion measures or standards that can be used in judging the extent to which actual outcomes conform to *their* standards and patients' expectations.

REFERENCES

1. Brown, C.R., Jr. and Uhl, H.S. Mandatory continuing education: Sense or nonsense. *J.A.M.A.*, Vol. 213, 1970, pp. 1660–1668.

2. Wandelt, M. *Guide for the Beginning Researcher.* New York: Appleton-Century-Crofts, 1970, p. 314.

This chapter was written with the collaboration of Helen V. Berg, Eleanor M. Brylski, Eileen E. Hilger, Helen J. Leary, Wilma Lewis, Rochelle J. Schmitz, Daleth A. Sparks, Dorothy Thompson, and Beverly E. Wolfgram.

Chapter 10

Analysis of Trends in Nursing Care Measurement

Barbara J. Stevens

Within the last ten years there has been great growth in the measuring, that is, quantifying, of nursing care. Ideally, if quantification can be done accurately, it should give a scientific base from which to solve many present nursing problems. For example, quantification should give a basis by which to *evaluate* whether care requirements have in fact been met, *relate* staffing patterns to care requirements, and *compare* the staffing patterns and quality of nursing care among institutions.

In actual practice, most quantification of nursing care has not yet reached a level at which it serves as a basis for decision making by administrators of nursing care. Indeed, many a director finds herself in the role of apologist when her institution fails to remain within the normal limits of some statewide or national survey of nursing hours per patient day. Every director of nursing care needs to have a good understanding of nursing measurement processes so that she can evaluate her own management abilities.

It is the position of this chapter that all measurement in nursing care should start with a quality control base. For example, it is unfair to compare the staffing needs of two hospitals on the basis of equal patient census when one hospital is located in a comfortable suburban setting while the other serves a ghetto population. The difference in basic teaching needs alone will radically increase nursing hours in the ghetto hospital, not to mention other factors such as concurrent health problems, lack of family resources, and so forth. Thus, measurement in nursing should start with the quality of care, not only because it is the primary aim in nursing, but because it is essential as a base upon which other meaningful measurements can be made.

Unfortunately, quality control has been the last, not the first, kind of measurement to be made. The reason is relatively simple: It is easier to count patients, nurses, or nursing tasks than it is to identify criteria upon which to determine quality levels. Quality control systems have begun to appear, how-

Reprinted with permission from "Analysis of Trends in Nursing Care Management" in *The Journal of Nursing Administration*, Volume 2, Number 2, November-December, 1972, pp. 1-6. © 1972.

ever, and their formulation will give the director of nursing care a base of support in assessing and justifying her support requirements for her institution's nursing care needs.

COMPONENTS OF A QUALITY CONTROL SYSTEM

What then comprises a nursing care quality control system? Slee identifies three essential components of any quality control program: (1) standards, (2) surveillance, and (3) corrective action[1]. The area of difficulty is the first, that of setting standards. One can choose to appraise any of the following: (1) structure, (2) process, and (3) outcome[2]. If one looks at the format of most accrediting agencies, such as the ANA, the NLN, and the JCAH, it is apparent that these groups have selected structure as the area of concern. The following questions or statements compiled from these three sources will illustrate the point:

1. Is a registered nurse responsible for planning, evaluating, and supervising the nursing care of each patient?
2. Are written care plans used?
3. The nursing department provides training programs and opportunities for staff development.
4. There is a system for recording accurate and objective observations of patients in the clinical record.

These questions and statements identify necessary, but not sufficient, criteria for quality care. Thus it might be necessary for a registered nurse to plan patient care, but because such care is planned by a registered nurse is no assurance that the planning is in fact well done. Written care plans may be necessary for good care, but that such plans are written does not, in and of itself, assure

that they are good plans. Criteria based on structure give conditions under which it is likely that good nursing care could take place, but such criteria do not assure that the good care does in fact take place.

Criteria based on outcomes would be ideal, but such criteria are difficult to identify at the present developmental level of nursing research. To use outcomes as criteria, one would have to be able to determine how much of the patient's return to wellness was due to nursing and how much was due to medicine. Documentation is available for intensive coronary nursing care,[3] but little is presently available for the bulk of nursing being done. Some interesting and encouraging data are being developed at health maintenance clinics where selected patient groups are divided between physician and nurse clinics[4]. Generally, however, it appears that nursing outcomes, as standards for quality measurement, will be useful only to nursing divisions operating on a high level of sophistication.

Thus the last criteria to be considered, that of process, offers the most realistic area in which to locate quality control. Many interesting things are presently being done to measure the nursing process. The director of nursing care should, however, be aware of two distinct forms of analysis, each of which has a different approach and a different aim.

TASK ANALYSIS METHOD

Early in the development of quality control, once nurse leaders had identified process as the area from which to develop quality criteria, there was a great tendency to call in the outside expert to develop the criteria by which to analyze the nursing process. This use of outside personnel, usually systems analysts, led to a task-oriented time analysis route of investigation. The experts, by using time studies, were able to establish time norms for most common nursing tasks. Note, however, that these norms were specific for the institution under investigation. Thus the average bathing time in a research hospital with critically ill patients might logically be longer than that in an average community hospital.

Nevertheless, such studies were of practical value in establishing some criteria for distribution of staff or patients. Nurses have always known that the same unit of thirty patients may be extremely busy one month and not so busy the next month, but never before have they had a scientific base as a distribution criterion. Such time studies usually revealed that certain tasks were significant in determining patient nursing care hours and that certain tasks were inconsequential. Drug distribution, for example, seldom affected patient care hours, while presence of a levine tube usually was related directly to increased nursing care hours.

Time studies have contributed greatly to improvements in patient care and staff placement, but certain inherent limitations should be noted. Since most of these original studies were formulated by systems persons rather than by nurses, a great emphasis was placed upon analysis and allocation of specific tasks to specific levels of nursing personnel. Such systems seldom left room, for example, for the patient who needed a registered nurse instead of a nursing assistant because of a high anxiety level (anxiety is not a task). Such studies, also, usually ignored the human need for continuity. If a patient required four levels of activities, then four separate persons should do those tasks.

The primary weakness of these studies, however, is that their data base was always the present practice. Tasks were timed as they actually took place rather than as they ought to have taken place. Thus these studies must be seen as descriptive rather than as prescriptive of nursing practice.

Studies utilizing the task analysis method are becoming more sophisticated. Certain computerized forms can now handle hundreds of specific nursing tasks, and many now include such hard-to-define tasks as patient teaching or relieving patient anxiety. Most nursing divisions have now established their own patient ranking system, usually based on selected tasks to be performed. The PETO system is one such development[5]. This method assigns point values to selected nursing tasks and selected patient states such as: (1) turning every hour rates 12 points, and (2) incontinence with average output rates 8 points. After all criteria have been rated and added, each patient's point value is converted into an estimated number of hours of nursing care. Such systems are extremely useful in patient care and staff placement, but they cannot perform a quality control function.

QUALITY CONTROL METHOD

A true nursing quality control system must (1) identify the desired nursing practice criteria, (2) establish a system for comparing the actual nursing practice to that criteria, and (3) use process standards rather than structure standards. The desired nursing practice criteria does not have to be defined in terms of the ideal: it may be defined in terms of the acceptable level of practice. Indeed, criteria can be developed to identify different levels of excellence in practice.

The primary difference between process and structure standards can be demonstrated by reviewing some of the previous structure standards and converting them to process standards.

Structure sample 2:   Are written care plans used?

Related process sample: Is the written care plan appropriate for the patient? Does it demonstrate consideration of his personal needs, disease-related needs, and therapy-related needs?

Structure sample 4: There is a system for recording accurate and objective observations of patients in the clinical record.

Related process sample: The charting shows evidence of relevant observations of patient progress, of patient response to therapy, and of completion of physician's orders. Evidence of the patient's psychic state is also present where relevant.

A critical difference between the structure standard and the process standard is that the process standard requires a professional judgment in determining whether each criterion has been met. This element of judgment does afford possibility for some differences in rating, but such differences can be decreased by writing each criterion in clearly defined behavioral terms.

The first step in establishing a quality control system is to identify the areas to be evaluated. These areas may be limited to direct patient care or may be expanded to cover other nursing functions such as recording, assigning, or maintaining equipment. The scope should depend upon the objectives and needs of the institution. Since the evaluating process may be time consuming, quality control is often limited to the evaluation of patient care alone rather than including nursing administrative functions. Another frequent pattern is to individualize a quality control form to cover all the nursing functions and patient care functions indigenous to a particular unit. A third possibility is that of developing quality control forms specific for particular patients. For example, one could devise a quality control form applicable to all patients with cardiovascular accidents.

Once the scope of the quality control has been determined, a general format for the form itself must be prepared. Since the format will influence the wording of the standards, it must be determined first. The principal rule to follow in selecting a format is to keep it simple, easy to use, and easily interpreted by all users. Some common formats are:

1.

Standards	Met	Unmet	Not observed	Comments
Long-range goals written on kardex				

2.

Standards	Excellent	Good	Fair	Poor	Not applicable

3.	Standards	1	2	3	4	5

4.	Standards	Above average	Average	Below average

5.	Standards category	First descriptive statement	Second descriptive statement	Third descriptive statement
	Patient teaching	Patient has received no teaching	Patient has received some teaching, but does not adequately understand material	Patient has received thorough teaching and understands what was taught

Form 1 is less likely to produce diverse opinions among raters; however, each standard must be defined precisely. Form 2 has the disadvantage of showing greater variation among raters. Form 3 has the same disadvantage, but may be useful if the institution wants to quantify the answers. Quantification has the advantage of promoting competition among nursing units or of permitting the nursing unit to strive to top its previous grade. Form 4 has the advantage of stability, for as the "average" improves in the institution, the form is still applicable. Form 5 is the most difficult to construct, but permits identification of specific levels of nursing care.

SOURCES OF EVIDENCE

Once the scope and format of the quality control system have been determined, the next step is to identify the sources of evidence. Primary and secondary sources are usually combined, but where possible, primary sources are preferable. A primary source gives the rater direct knowledge concerning the standard. For example, if a standard is, "Patient receives adequate oral hygiene," the rater goes to the source, the patient, to observe for this standard. For the standard, "Emergency equipment is complete and ready for use," the observer again goes directly to the source, i.e., evaluates the equipment firsthand.

Not all standards lend themselves to immediate observation techniques. "Promotion of independence" might require a careful evaluation of nursing notes over a period of time. Some standards may combine primary and secondary sources. For example, "Adequate hydration is maintained," might combine direct observation of the skin turgor with secondary observation of the intake and output records.

The patient's chart is a frequent secondary source. Indeed, the evaluation of nursing via the chart is often either included in the quality check or developed separately as a nursing chart audit. Another source often used is the patient's response of satisfaction or dissatisfaction with his nursing care. It is important that a group forming a quality control check determine ahead how relevant patient satisfaction is as evidence of professional care. Wording of questions to patients is quite important. Some questions can be worded so as to give primary responses: "Did the nurse discuss your surgery with you the day before the operation?" Others cannot be given similar weight: "Are you generally pleased with your nursing care?" The following sources are those most frequently used in quality control checks: charts, rounds, records, nursing care plans, patient interviews, nurse interviews, interviews of other health personnel.

After sources of evidence have been selected, the final step in the process is that of constructing the relevant standards. As mentioned previously, the standards should be given in precise behavioral terms so that each rater will give the statement or question the same interpretation. Another factor to consider is proportion. For example, there should not be twice as many questions on psychological aspects as on physical aspects of care unless the group considers psychological aspects twice as important as physical aspects. Thus one should aim for a balanced checklist, with emphasis only on those areas identified as extremely important.

FACTORS THAT INFLUENCE THE QUALITY CONTROL SYSTEM

Many other issues may influence both the quality control form and the implementation policy. The director of nursing care needs to clearly define her purposes for using a quality control system. Formation and implementation of a quality control system can be an educative experience for supervisors and head nurses. If staff development is one of the primary objectives of the quality control system, then the staff should develop its own system. A group can learn much by devising, revising, and testing its own evaluation tool.

If, however, the director is more interested in accurate patient care feedback, then she may wish to have a form evolved with more expertise. Another valid purpose for the quality control system is that of serving as a motivator toward better patient care. Competitive factors have already been discussed. The quality control system also is useful in spotting areas of general weakness and thus may be used as a diagnostic tool by staff education departments.

Still another factor that will influence the form of the quality control system is the department's concept of nursing. The following samples represent divisions of patient care which could be used as a basis for structuring a quality control form.

1. Nursing care[6]
   a. Sustenal
   b. Remedial
   c. Restorative
   d. Preventive
2. Nursing problems[7]
   a. Preserve body defenses
   b. Prevent complications
   c. Reestablish patient with outside world

    d. Detect changes in the body's regulatory system

    e. Implement prescribed therapeutic and diagnostic activity

    f. Provide comfort

3. Nursing care as process[8]

    a. Observation

    b. Inference

    c. Validation

    d. Assessment

    e. Action

    f. Evaluation

The particular structure selected is not as important as that a structure *be* selected. Too many control checklists lack organization and simply present a random list of standards.

Finally, after a form is completed, it is important to implement its use in a systematic way. One needs to determine who will evaluate what at what times. Answers to these questions must be based on the institution's needs, but the following guidelines have proved useful in many organizations.

1. Schedule evaluation visits at periodic, but unannounced intervals. The surprise visit is more likely to reflect the normal pattern of nursing care.

2. Not all patients need be evaluated; a sampling technique is quite satisfactory.

3. Patient sampling may be done at random, or patients may be selected on the basis of those requiring challenging nursing care.

4. Persons should serve on the evaluation team long enough to become thoroughly familiar with the evaluation process.

5. If evaluation members split the work, each member should grade the *same* portion of the checklist on all units evaluated.

	Task Analysis System	Quality Control System
Aim of system	Fairly distribute nursing tasks	Evaluate the quality of care
Basic criterion	What *is* being done	What *ought* to be done
Concept of nursing	Nursing is a series of specific tasks	Nursing is process (there is room for various different theories)
What the system points out	Instances when a team produces less completed tasks than the norm	Instances of exceptional nursing, both good and bad
Perspective	What happens in the care delivery system	What happens to the patient

USE OF QUALITY CONTROL DATA

The third area of quality control identified by Slee was that of corrective action. A quality control system is useless if proper and immediate feedback is not offered to the nursing units involved. It is, however, more productive to have the staff view quality control as a challenge than as a club over their heads. Supervisors and head nurses can be counseled to see the program as a diagnostic tool more easily if they have an integral part in its operation.

For the director, a measure of the quality of nursing care gives a scientific basis upon which to calculate needed nursing personnel. She can measure the point at which increased staffing alone fails to improve care quality. Likewise, she has data to support the point at which care begins to decline due to personnel shortages. The quality control system, as opposed to the time study task analysis approach, has another advantage: it identifies instances when particular nursing teams are more productive of good care than are similar circumstances. Thus it may recognize appropriate nursing models for study and imitation. The task analysis method defines all nurses at interchangeable integers. While it will indicate failures of a nursing team to carry the expected number of tasks, it has no means of identifying group excellence in care.

The graph compares some of the critical differences in purpose between the two systems.

Another factor which makes quality control data even more important is the present financial crisis in health institutions. The director of nursing care is in the difficult position of trying to interpret good nursing care to non-nurse administrators who make decisions vitally affecting nursing resources. Under present economic conditions, administrators may feel justified in decreasing nursing personnel as long as "the job still gets done." Quality control data can help make visible to the non-nurse administrator the price that is paid in such instances. Quality control data provides a guide to staffing needs based upon the quality of nursing care rather than upon less critical issues.

REFERENCES

1. Slee, V.N. How to know if you have quality control. *Hosp. Progr.*, Vol. 53, No. 1, 1972, pp. 38–43.
2. Donabedian, A. Some issues in evaluating the quality of nursing care. *Amer. J. Public Health*, Vol. 59, No. 10, 1969, p. 1833.
3. Meltzer, L.E. CCU's can save thousands of lives; nurse is key factor in success. *Hosp. Topics*, Vol. 49, No. 9, 1971, pp. 26–27.
4. Lewis, C., and Resnik, B. Nurse clinics and progressive ambulatory care. *New Engl. J. Med.*, Vol. 277, No. 23, 1967, p. 1236.
5. Poland, M., et al. PETO—A system for assessing and meeting patient care needs. *Amer. J. Nurs.*, Vol. 70, No. 7, 1970, p. 1479.
6. Pardee, G., et al. Patient care evaluation is every nurse's job. *Amer. J. Nurs.*, Vol. 71, No. 10, 1971, p. 1958.
7. Brodt, D.E. A synergistic theory of nursing. *Amer. J. Nurs.*, Vol. 69, No. 8, 1969, p. 1674.
8. Carrieri, V., and Sitzman, J. Components of nursing process. *Nurs. Clinics of N. Amer.*, Vol. 6, No. 1, 1971, pp. 115–121.

UNIT III

NURSING PROCESS, NURSING STANDARDS AND QUALITY CONTROL

Introduction

In the past, nurses tended to verbalize maximal standards of patient care, which in practice they could not achieve. This led to a considerable amount of frustration for nurses and, in fact, promoted reluctance to evaluate nursing care. Lack of evaluation, in turn, promoted the continuance of unrealistic standards setting. As a result, nurses did not, and in many settings still do not, set realistic standards of care. They also continue to find evaluation programs threatening and resist them in a variety of ways. This situation surely cannot persist in the face of the present requirements of federally legislated quality assurance programs. All health care providers will be required to identify standards and show how their own input is related to achievement of the standards. Nurses will find it necessary to set realistic standards of nursing care and utilize effective quality control and evaluation methods to ensure that the standards are achieved and if not, show that appropriate action was taken to change the standard or to change the care to achieve it.

Previous units of this book identified processes and terminology relevant to standard setting and to quality assurance programs, and cited the more important factors that influence the standards set by nurses. This unit focuses on the setting of standards and devising of quality control mechanisms in the context of the nursing process. Nicholls's chapter is addressed to the introduction of quality control into nursing care planning and practice. Identification of standards, development of information feedback systems, and action planned to ensure the achievement of standards as part of nursing process are described.

Wessells's chapter defines her concept of the components of nursing process and elaborates on subprocesses within each component. By means of a sample case, she illustrates how to derive broad standards, specific outcomes, and feedback systems, and how to use them for control and evaluation.

Klein and Wessells use a sample case to demonstrate standard setting by a multidisciplinary group for an individual client, and identify some of the difficulties encountered in establishing that the input of any one discipline had a crucial impact on the outcomes of care.

Chapter 11

Quality Control in Patient Care

Marion E. Nicholls

A natural outcome of public dissatisfaction and nationwide demands for change in the whole field of health care is that each profession faces the need to establish its value in terms of quality, availability, and cost. Politicians, spokesmen for professional organizations, social planners, and citizens' groups are all espousing one plan or another to lower the cost of health care and to distribute it more equitably.

Nursing literature describes many efforts to define the nurse's role more clearly[1-3], and to devise tools for evaluating the quality of nursing care[4-6]. The American Nurses' Association has published "Standards of Nursing Practice" and revised "Standards for Nursing Services." Role definition, however, seems to be taking place primarily in theory while actual practice keeps changing in response to other forces in the practice setting. Nursing care planning, a primary source of standards for nursing care, is used faithfully as a teaching tool, much less frequently in practice. Evaluation of patient care is often transmuted into agency evaluation of employee performance.

Several quality control programs have been initiated by hospital nursing administrators in recent years[7, 8]. The analysis of tasks has been used for some time to determine staffing patterns. Unfortunately, task analysis also has become the basis for many quality control programs. The major drawback in doing this, as Barbara Stevens points out, is that, while task analysis "will indicate failures of a nursing team to carry the expected number of tasks, it has no means of identifying group excellence in care"[9]. When nursing care is reduced to a series of activities, it becomes feasible, at least theoretically, to train a variety of workers to carry out blocks of tasks. This could be viewed by hospital administrators as one solution to a hospital's economic problems. The administrator might justify his decision with data indicating that "x" number of tasks was accomplished by personnel less expensive than nurses. In reality these data re-

Reprinted with permission from *American Journal of Nursing*, Volume 74, Number 3, March, 1974, pp. 456–459. © 1974 The American Journal of Nursing Company.

flect only the numbers of tasks completed, not the quality of patient care rendered.

Process was proposed by Stevens as the most realistic area for quality control. She indicates that quality control based on outcomes would be ideal, but she says that the lack of sufficient data based on sound research means that "nursing outcomes, as standards for quality measurement, will be useful only to nursing divisions operating on a high level of sophistication"[10]. The advantage Stevens sees in quality control based on process is that it requires "professional judgment in determining whether each criterion has been met"[11].

Although process has been substituted for task, the emphasis continues to be on what the nurse does to the patient rather than on the quality of care he receives. In either the task-analysis or the process-oriented quality control system, the standards tend to be developed at the administrative level. The degree to which practitioners agree with the standards determines the support they will give to the program. If the practitioner does not view quality control as an integral part of practice, then she may well see administratively initiated quality control programs as agency-imposed evaluation of her performance.

If quality control is to be product oriented (that is, control of the quality of the total nursing care that is received by the patient) rather than performance oriented, it must be perceived by practitioners as an integral part of all nursing care, not just a periodic departmental evaluation. Planning patient care, whether formalized in writing or not, has generally been accepted by nurses as part of their professional responsibility. To practice quality control, we must make a similar commitment to building it into our plans.

For many persons, unfortunately, "control" evokes ideas of restriction, limitation, and even coercion. Dictionary definitions do include such words as "direct, regulate, dominate." However, in daily life, we control a whole range of activities. The baker controls the baking process by testing the consistency of a cake at timed intervals. Failure to control an automobile by constant adjustment of direction and speed can be disastrous. Control activities that nurses regularly accept are maintaining narcotic records, recording administration of medications, and, in some situations, keeping records that serve as controls for other departments.

In nursing care planning and implementation, control is essential whether the nurse gives the care or manages it. Few nurses provide direct care on a twenty-four-hour basis. Most practitioners in hospitals today combine direct intervention with management of the care provided by other staff. For managers of nursing care, control is an essential component of the management operation.

Control, according to Douglas Sherwin, is "action which adjusts operations to predetermined standards, and its basis is information in the hands of managers"[12]. This definition has three components: a standard, an information feedback system, and an action taken to keep performance in line with the standard. In patient care, the standards for control are found in the nursing care plan. As a plan changes in response to a patient's needs, the standards, feedback system, and actions to maintain performance also change. Quality control in direct nursing care does not call for elaborate changes in planning and carrying out nursing care. Primarily, control requires that nurses become more conscious of standards and more adept in devising and using information-feedback systems.

Nursing care planning begins with an assessment of a patient's problems and the resources to solve them. Assessment yields facts about the patient and the resources,

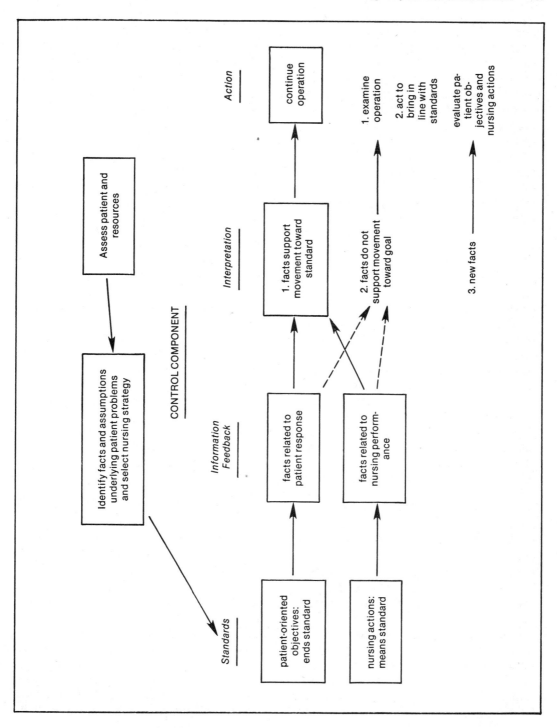

and leads to assumptions about the appropriate nursing strategy to initiate. The next steps are to identify patient-oriented objectives and the plan of nursing care that will help him achieve his objectives. When stated correctly, the objectives and the written plan become the standards for a quality control system (see diagram). Addition of an identified information-feedback system and the resultant action to maintain the nursing care in line with the standards constitute quality control of the nursing plan and its implementation.

STANDARDS

Nursing care standards can be divided into ends and means standards. The ends standards are patient oriented; they describe the changes desired in a patient's physical status or behavior. The means standards are nurse oriented; they describe the activities and behavior designed to achieve the ends standards. Properly stated, nursing care objectives are the ends standards and the plan of care (or nursing orders) is the means standard. Although the ends and means standards are interrelated, different information about each is required to determine if they are being met. An ends standard requires information about the patient. A means standard calls for information about the nurse's performance. To be effective as standards, objectives and plans must meet three criteria. The statements must be understandable. They must be achievable in terms of the resources of the patient, the nurses, and the agency. And, if control is to be achieved, they must be measurable.

Clarity as a criterion requires a standard that anyone of average intelligence and familiarity with the terminology can understand. Abstract, ambiguous standards may create a haven for the insecure practitioner but they also make it difficult to prove

actual accomplishment. For example, an objective (ends standard) that is unclear is "Patient will accept his diagnosis." Proof that he had achieved this goal might be a report that the patient said he had "x" disease, but one would suspect that this was not the intent of the standard.

A more appropriate statement would be "The patient will make plans that include appropriate modifications in goals, activities, and behaviors required by the impact of the health problem and its treatment." For a specific patient, the actual modifications would be specified. A nursing intervention that cannot serve as a standard is "Provide emotional support." How could one determine what behaviors of the nurse met the standard unless it was clear what constituted "emotional support" for a particular patient?

Achievability requires that a standard fall within the capabilities of the patient, the nursing department, and the agency resources to accomplish it. An ends standard such as "The patient will be able to carry out activities of daily living before discharge from the hospital" sounds reasonable for someone who is a recent hemiplegic. If, however, the patient is in a 60-bed hospital with a limited physical therapy department and an unstable nursing staff, it is probably an unachievable standard. More achievable objectives (ends standards) might be "The patient will maintain muscle strength and will be aware of community resources to help him continue his rehabilitation program."

Some patient factors to consider in setting achievable standards include his physical and mental capacity, emotional readiness, financial resources, and family support. The nursing resources to assess are the knowledge and competence of the nurses, their degree of authority, time constraints, staffing patterns, and so forth. The agency resources include, among others, the availability of equipment, allied clinical departments, and financial status.

Measurability, the third criterion, implies that information can be collected to determine whether the standard has been met. The standard must be specific in describing outcomes, the means to achieve the outcomes, and the time for accomplishment. An ends standard that would not meet these requirements is "The patient will know about diabetes." At one extreme in knowledge of diabetes is a medical specialization in the field; at the other end may be a vague concept of the disorder and perhaps some skill in administering insulin. It is difficult to say what information would be needed to determine whether the standard had been met. A more measurable standard would identify the level of knowledge of diabetes and the measures to control it that a patient could verbalize and demonstrate before discharge.

The time limits are also essential. Unless there is joint planning with a community agency, the nurse in a hospital can set standards only for her period of contact with the patient. Even within that period of time, standards must be changed on the basis of the patient's current status. Standards that are no longer relevant are useless, and cannot be used to measure accomplishment.

INFORMATION FEEDBACK

The difference between control and evaluation is important because information feedback has impact on both. The decision that a particular ends standard is desirable and that a certain means standard will be instituted is based on facts and assumptions derived from assessing a situation and identifying an existing problem. Litchfield states that "a decision which has been programmed, communicated, and controlled has validity only for the limited period in which the facts, assumptions, and values upon which it was

based have retained their original character"[13]. When an objective has been achieved, the facts are no longer the same. Since control is operationally oriented and based on the identified standards, then the standard determines how long the control system operates and the information to be obtained. Once the type of information has been identified, the method of obtaining it becomes obvious.

An example of an ends standard for a patient with a decubitus ulcer is "The ulcer will show evidence of healing in a week." The obvious information needed to determine if the standard is being met includes the amount of drainage, size and depth of the ulcer, degree of redness, amount of swelling, and so on. To say "the ulcer is improving" is a waste of time. A description of its diameter in inches or in comparison to some common object like a coin is necessary. Since more than one person cares for the patient, precise information is necessary to measure progress toward the goal.

The question might arise: why set up an information feedback system on performance if the information about the patient indicates that satisfactory progress is being made toward the objective (ends standard)?

Feedback on performance is necessary to maintain accountability for nursing performance toward the achievement of the objective (ends standard).

If a patient fails to progress toward the objective, feedback is required to determine whether this is due to failure of the means or to failure of the lan. If the means standard is not being met, action must be taken. When an objective (ends standard) is shared by medicine and nursing, a failure to meet a means standard in nursing can be overcome through medical intervention. For example, an objective for a postoperative patient might be "to have adequate fluid intake on a clear liquid diet." If the nursing means standard "to offer 100 cc fluid per hour and increase as tolerated" was not met, the physician might order intravenous fluids. The objective (ends standard) of adequate fluid intake was achieved but the nursing means standard was not met.

Information feedback on performance should be precise, but not require extensive record keeping. Reports, checklists, records, nursing notes, and observed performance all serve as routes for information feedback. The important aspect is that the information required is clearly identified. Feedback about a teaching plan, for instance, would include the actual content of the teaching session and the patient's response. Nursing tasks repeated at frequent intervals might require a bedside checklist.

MAINTAINING PERFORMANCE

Action to maintain performance in line with standards is the third component of control. There are three possible courses of action in response to information feedback. First, if the information indicates progress toward the objective (ends standard) and the performance is in line with the means standard, no action is required. Second, if progress toward the ends standard is too slow or not effective, the actual performance of nursing care must be measured against the means standard. If the performance standards are not being met, then action must be taken to improve performance. Some actions that may be taken are to determine if the performance standards are known and understood, to identify and deal with any factors that may prevent appropriate performance, and to reinterpret standards. If the performance standard is being met but the ends standard is not, then an evaluation of both ends and means standards is necessary. The facts on which the nursing care plan was built may have been incorrectly assessed, or they may have changed. A new plan with an appropriate control system must be devised.

The nursing department administrator is responsible for the quality of nursing care within a department and must develop quality control programs to determine if standards are being met. Departmental quality control programs should gain acceptance and be more effective if there is meaningful input from practitioners who practice control in direct nursing care.

An effective control program is one in which the participants identify the ends and means standards and provide information to indicate whether they are being met. All members of the staff should view control as a means of determining whether the goals accepted by the staff are being achieved. Individual performance may be identified as a factor in failure to achieve a standard, but assessment of individual performance should not be the main thrust of control in nursing care. Individual staff evaluation should be a concomitant but separate program.

True quality control in planning and giving nursing care can help ensure that nursing care meets patients' objectives. To do this, all members of the nursing staff will need to share in developing standards and in devising and using information feedback systems.

REFERENCES

1. U.S. Health, Education, and Welfare Department, Secretary's Committee to Study Extended Roles for Nurses. Extending the scope of nursing practice. *Am. J. Nurs.* Vol. 71, Dec. 1971, pp. 2346–2351.

2. Nursing at the crossroads. *Nurs. Outlook*, Jan. 1972.

3. Cleland, V. Implementation of change in health care systems. *J. Nurs. Admin.*, Vol. 2, Nov.-Dec. 1972, pp. 64–69.

4. Bidwell, C.M. and Froebe, D.J. Development of an instrument for evaluating hospital nursing performance. *J. Nurs. Admin.*, Vol. 1, Sept.-Oct. 1971, pp. 10–15.

5. Albrecht, S. Reappraisal of conventional performance appraisal systems. *J. Nurs. Educ.,* Vol. 2, Mar.-Apr. 1972, pp. 29–35.

6. Rubin, C.F. Nursing audit-nurses evaluating nursing. *Am. J. Nurs.*, Vol. 72, May 1972, pp. 916–921.

7. McGuire, R.L. Bedside nursing audit. *Am. J. Nurs.*, Vol. 68, Oct. 1968, pp. 2146–2148.

8. O'Malley, C.E. Application of systems engineering in nursing. *Am. J. Nurs.*, Vol. 69, Oct. 1969,

9. Stevens, B.J. Analysis of trends in nursing care management. *J. Nurs. Admin.*, Vol. 2, Nov.-Dec. 1972, p. 12.

10. Stevens, B.J., p. 17.

11. Stevens, B.J. p. 14.

12. Sherwin, D.S. "The meaning of control" in *The Nature and Scope of Management*, M.S. Wadia, (ed.), Chicago: Scott, Foresman and Co., 1966, p. 203.

13. Litchfield, E. "Notes on a general theory of administration" in *The Nature and Scope of Management*, M.S. Wadia, (ed.),. Chicago: Scott, Foresman and Co., 1966, p. 28.

Chapter 12

Nursing Process and Quality Control

Virginia G. Wessells

Nursing process is a most important part of management of nursing care of individual clients and families. It is focused on the clinical care of the client/family, but does not embrace all aspects of nursing management. Some aspects of nursing management not covered in nursing process are: assignment, supervision, and teaching of auxiliary nursing personnel; the setting of standards for and evaluation of the care of large groups of clients; the acquisition and use of nonpeople resources; the preparation, execution, and evaluation of quality control programs. Nursing process, then, is not all of nursing management, but is a crucial part of it.

Nursing process is a series of activities utilized by nurses to fulfill the clinical purposes of nursing. These activities are dynamic and interrelated, and consist of five major phases. They are diagrammed in static relationship to one another in Figure 1. The action is shown to progress in clockwise fashion, but in reality the process is more dynamic than this. Back and forth movement or reverse action may (and often does) occur, so that there is a return to the pre-

vious phase or series of phases to accommodate for new information or for a change in the client's condition or situation.

Each phase in nursing process, except nursing diagnosis, is composed of multiple activities and is actually a process in itself. Nursing diagnosis is viewed as a single activity—that of listing/describing the client's problems as they concern nursing.

Nursing process is composed of direct care activities (execution) and indirect care activities (assessment, planning, diagnosis, and evaluation). The major focus of this essay will be on the indirect care activities in nursing process, and on quality control as used in the execution phase to obtain the necessary feedback for ongoing operations and for evaluation purposes. Particular attention will be paid to the impact of nursing care on the outcome of the client's total care.

THE MAJOR PHASES OF NURSING PROCESS

The action for client care in nursing rests on two bases—identifying the client's problems and deciding which of those problems should be acted upon by nursing at this time. One begins with a nursing assessment.

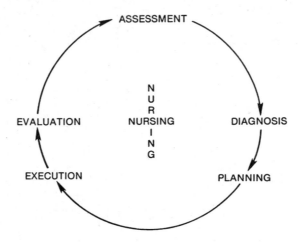

FIGURE 1.   NURSING PROCESS—THE FIVE MAJOR PHASES

Nursing Assessment

Nursing assessment is the gathering and analysis of data preliminary to identification of the nursing diagnosis. Nursing assessment includes:

A. Data Collection
   (1) Collection of data concerning the client's identified problems.
   (2) Investigation of unidentified/suspected problems.
   (3) The uncovering of information relevant to:
      a. Maintenance of the client's health.
      b. His adaptive capabilities.
      c. Other problems (preventative or restorative) of concern to nursing.

B. The Inference Process
   (1) Examination of all of the data available.
   (2) Selection of pertinent data for current use, and disposal of remaining data.
   (3) Review of all of the client's problems—known and suspected.
   (4) Consideration of the interrelatedness of various problems and solutions in process.
   (5) The matching of problem solutions to the resources available to the client.
   (6) Estimations of the capability of nursing to resolve or assist the client to resolve the problems.

C. Drawing of Tentative Conclusions (based on all of the preceding activity in phases A and B)

Sources of data. As she initiates nursing process, the nurse seeks out sources of data; these range from many to few depending upon her location. The most common sources of data in any setting might include the client and his family; multiple health care providers, including students; old and new medical records; diagnostic testing data; visitors, friends, minister, colleagues, employer, and others. When large volumes of data are available, the use of abstracts or summaries helps reduce time and energy expenditure. In the future, it may be common for data retrieval systems, with permission of the client, to print out health record accumulations for professional use. Longitudinal histories covering an individual's entire life will perhaps be compiled as well, and become a most valuable data source. At present the sources mentioned above are still the most commonly available.

Data collection. Data acquisition by the nurse often begins with a nursing history acquired through interview; it continues with assessment through observation of the client's physical appearance and immediate behavioral manifestations, and proceeds through physical examination appropriate to the setting and consistent with the level of knowledge and skill of the nurse. Thereafter, the decision about where or from whom to seek data could vary considerably depending upon the location of the client, the level of illness/wellness he is experiencing, the availability of family or significant others, the involvement/availability of other health personnel in the client's care, and other variables.

At times, the medical diagnosis and physician's orders and a cursory inspection of the patient are the sole data acquired prior to planning and execution of nursing care. Hopefully this is becoming less common, as preplanning of admission to an agency or practice improves, and as nurses become more cognizant of their independent professional responsibilities. With the sophistication of today's practice, the nurse should have access to, acquire, and utilize all the data necessary for professional-level decisions. Anything less is unacceptable and could result in legal prosecution for negligence or malpractice[1].

The influence of time and circumstance. The collection and selection of data and the immediacy of use are highly dependent upon the circumstances under which the nurse and client meet and upon the immediate restorative measures required to provide for the patient's safety. For example, the nurse may encounter a person who collapses unconscious on the sidewalk. Superficial observation suggests that the individual, who now becomes a client, has suffered a cardiopulmonary arrest (client is pale, inert, non-responsive, with no visible chest movement). Examination for readily palpable pulses and listening to the chest reveal no heartbeat or breath sounds, and no respiratory movement can be observed. At this point, the nurse must risk cardiopulmonary resuscitation or flee the scene. In other words, the data is collected and analyzed, action is selected and executed within five minutes, or it is useless to have the data since the patient can be expected to suffer irreversible brain damage, or death.

Nurses who work regularly in emergency rooms, with rescue squads, or in intensive care units are those most likely to have to make immediate decisions and initiate action on the basis of limited data. The variables of time and the immediate health requirements of the client, then, affect the amount of data available, the speed of processing, the use of data, and the course of decision making[2].

The broad goals shown in Figure 2 are those which commonly guide nursing action in acute care and in initial encounters with clients. They would not necessarily obtain in all settings or at all points on the continuum of client care.

The spiral effect. The sequence of action shown in Figure 2 signals the beginning of nursing process, which proceeds in spiral fashion thereafter. It is common for the nurse to begin application of the nursing process with limited data soon after encountering the client. She follows the process through the execution phase, but immediately begins revisions based on subsequent

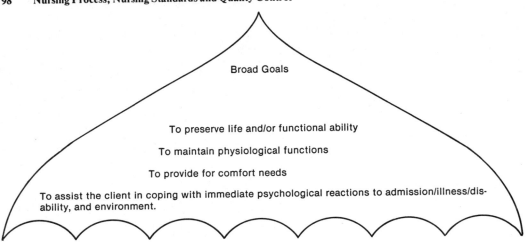

Broad Goals

To preserve life and/or functional ability

To maintain physiological functions

To provide for comfort needs

To assist the client in coping with immediate psychological reactions to admission/illness/disability, and environment.

Acute emergency care—sequence of events and action:

Initial encounter with client

Instant data collection (assessment) added to pertinent information acquired prior to encounter

Instant analysis

Decision for action to provide for broad goals (listed above)

Execution of action

FIGURE 2.   APPLICATION OF NURSING PROCESS IN THE EARLY STAGES OF CLIENT CARE

evaluation, reassessment, and incoming data. This cyclic activity continues as long as she provides care to the client. The nursing process diagrammed in Figure 1 depicts an ideal sequence of events; in reality, a spiral effect is more likely. Time limitations and the care requirements of the client(s) force the nurse to make and execute action decisions before the ideal sequence can occur.

The inference process. Under ideal circumstances, all available data would be collected, and then it would undergo examination, the first step in the inference process. After completing (or even before completing) the screening of the data, the nurse moves into the second phase—selecting data pertinent for use by nursing, and disposal/placement of the remaining data.

Whether the encounter is emergency-crisis, intermediate, or long-term care, the nurse would:

include

all data relevant for nursing purposes and necessary to set immediate short-term goals. Those that deal with threat to life, functional ability, and maintenance.

defer

data relevant to future decisions—store for future reference.

exclude

those data that can be immediately identified as nonrelevant for nursing purposes at this point in time.

omit

data inappropriate for use in the particular setting.

Selection and collation of data related to the client, his current status, and his potential for benefit from health care assistance feed into the intellectual process of inference—drawing conclusions based on the data. The nurse uses her knowledge of the basic sciences; the normal physio-psycho-social states of man, his adaptive processes and pathophysiological states; treatment possibilities and their preventive-maintenal-restorative potential in the inference process. The intellectual ability of the professional nurse to seek out problems, pursue solutions, and to make objective judgments about clients, families, and communities, plays a crucial role in the outcomes of the inference process.

Tentative conclusions are derived by 1) processing and analyzing the data through examination of all the client's care requirements and problems in a holistic frame of reference;* 2) considering the interrelatedness of the problems and the solutions in progress; and 3) "problem sorting" in which the resources available to resolve the client's problems are weighed against the appropriateness and potential effectiveness of nurse intervention to resolve each problem.

As the nursing process spirals on, with resulting changes and introduction of new data, the inference process proceeds. Inferences multiply and are often subjected to a validation process (sometimes requiring collection of more data) followed by conclusions related to the nature and scope of the client's problems with which nursing will

---

*"Man is a physiological-psycho-social being. To assail, ignore, or abridge any aspect of this integrated condition may impair the state of his health." Wessells, V. *Nursing History and Assessment of the Hospitalized Patient*, unpublished, 1973.

deal. When the nurse is ready to make even a tentative statement of the client's problems in this context, she has reached the diagnostic phase of nursing process.

Nursing Diagnosis

The nursing diagnosis is tentative in the early stages of client care, and becomes more clearly identified as the client progresses along the continuum of care. The nursing assessment phase of the nursing process is concluded when a firm nursing diagnosis is reached.

Nursing diagnosis is a listing or a description of the client's problems with which nursing can legitimately deal at a particular point in time.

When the nursing diagnosis is considered for interdisciplinary planning purposes, with diagnoses made by other groups it may again be revised and become more specific (Figure 3). It may change rapidly as the client progresses along the continuum of care. An accurate nursing diagnosis lays the foundation for decisions about appropriate action and for setting adequate standards for nursing care. These determinations, in turn, are an important and sometimes crucial contribution to the multidisciplinary plan of care.

An example of nursing diagnosis for a selected client is presented in Figure 4. The client involved is Ms. C., an 85-year-old black female admitted to a rehabilitation and extended care nursing home on July 22, 1974, with a medical diagnosis of:

Left hip nailing for intertrochanteric fracture of femur (8 days post-op.)
Cardiomegaly
Compensated congestive heart failure
Urinary tract infection (treated)
Decubitus ulcer of the sacrum, 3.5 cm × 3.5 cm, superficial in depth

Nurse Behavior in Response to Initial Encounter
with a Client for Elective Admission to a Hospital,
Nursing Home, or Extended Care Facility

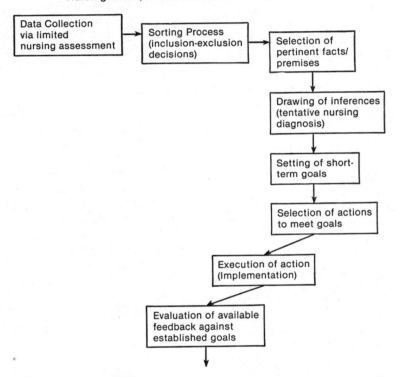

FIGURE 3.   NURSING PROCESS ON THE CONTINUUM OF NURSING CARE

Nurse behavior in a later phase of client encounter:

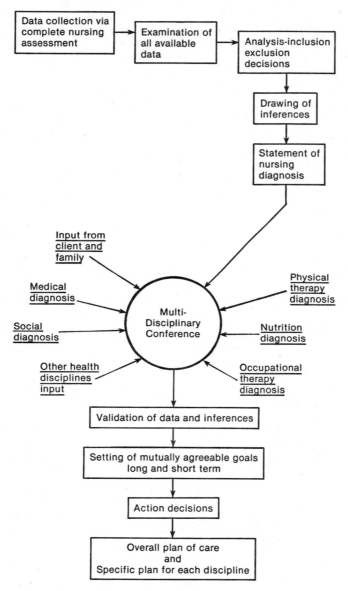

FIGURE 3 (continued). NURSING PROCESS ON THE CONTINUUM OF NURSING CARE

Maintenance Needs	Preventive Needs	Restorative Needs

Provision for assistance with:
Food
Drink
Sleep
Elimination
Cleanliness and warmth
Safety
Exercise & weight bearing
Meaningful activity
Diversion
Social interaction
Self actualization
Love
Self-esteem
Status
Recognition
	Prevention of:
	Muscle atrophy/weakness
	Emotional/mental depression
	  and confusion
	Loss of self-esteem
	Loss of ability to perform
	  activities of daily living
	Recurrence of urinary tract
	  infection
	Bone demineralization
		Promotion of:
		Healing of fractured hip
		  bone
		Independence in activities
		  of daily living
		Heal decubitus

Specific problems related to the aforestated needs of Ms. C. (Nursing Diagnosis)

1. Drinks less than 2,400 ccs per day.	1. Needs opportunity to perform at maximum in activities of daily living.	1. Unable to ambulate normally—must refrain from weight bearing on (L) leg.
2. Bowel movements do not occur at regular times, therefore require special treatment and scheduling.	2. Needs ambulation, transfer activity, and muscle maintenance and strengthening exercise.	2. Must keep weight off (L) leg during transfers.
3. Unable to perform all of hygienic care and dressing activities: Unable to reach back and legs for washing and dressing purposes. Unable to fasten back ties and buttons. Requires assist with grooming of hair and nails.	3. Dislikes being dependent. 4. Wants to be home but has no one to live with to assist with maintenal care.	3. Insufficient knowledge of nonweight-bearing transfer procedure.
4. Does not know how to effect safe, nonweight-bearing transfers. Forgets to lock wheelchair.	5. Her children do not provide much attention or assistance.	4. Cleansing and observation of decubitus— supervision of care of same.
5. Partially deaf—no hearing aid. Communication is difficult.	6. Requires observation and supervision of urinary elimination.	

FIGURE 4.   NURSING DIAGNOSIS FOR MS. C.

After the rehabilitation team was consulted, medical orders were issued:

(1) *No weight bearing on the left leg.*
(2) Up in the wheel chair *ad lib.*
(3) Ambulate in parallel bars with supervision (Physical Therapy) five times weekly.
(4) May use commode or bathroom after instructions in nonweight-bearing transfer.
(5) Regular diet.
(6) Force fluids.
(7) Aspirin gr. X every 4 hours, p.r.n. for pain in hip.
(8) Occupational Therapy activity to maintain muscle strength and provide for diversional needs.

In Figure 4, the nursing diagnosis for this patient is diagrammed according to the three major categories of client need at that point in time.

Nursing Care Planning

The nursing care plan is composed of aims and actions designed to solve the problems identified in the nursing diagnosis, and includes the setting of standards within the framework of the identified aims and actions. These standards encompass establishment of priorities for action and the minimal safe standard of care for both the individual client and the group of clients being served, since sharing of resources is required in most settings.

In client-centered health care, client is involved in the care planning process from the initial contact onward. The family members may or may not be involved, depending on the circumstances and the wishes of the client. In the event of catastrophic/emergency illness, the client's family or some other persons may become the client's advocate and enter into the decision-making

process if the client is unable to do so. This is particularly true when life-threatening events occur, and the client cannot make decisions. Under these conditions, the health care providers may become the major decision makers.

Goal setting. The setting of broad goals for client care precedes the identification of actions and the predictions of specific outcomes. These derive from (a) the philosophy-purpose-objectives of the agency/practice, (b) mutual agreement between client and provider about problems to be solved, (c) the resources available to achieve the goals, and (d) the realistic outcomes desired by the client and his family. These broad goals are useful as directional guides—they keep redirecting us when questions and deviations occur. They assist us as planning proceeds and progress is made toward the identification of more specific goals and specific desired outcomes. They also help us maintain our focus on the client in a holistic frame of reference. They are not especially helpful in the measurement of the quality of the health care provided, because they are too broad for measurement purposes. (See examples in Figure 5.)

The orderly progression of care rests in part on the preadmission screening of the client. This activity permits consideration of the client's already identified needs and problems and the institution's potential for resolving these. The institution's broad goals must be consistent with the broad goals set for each specific client. (See Figure 5).

The goals shown in Figure 5 are a portion of the means standards* for the specific client—Ms. C. Note that the goals become more specific as they progress from left to right.

---

*The means standard for an individual client includes the broad goals and nursing actions identified to resolve the client's problem(s), condition(s), or situation.

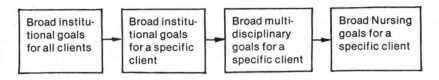

The Nursing Home— Overall goals	The Nursing Home— Goals for the care of Ms. C.	Multidisciplinary— Goals for the care of Ms. C.	Nursing— Goals for the care of Ms. C.
To provide for maintenal care needs of all clients: Environment (room, heating, lighting) Housekeeping (cleanliness) Food Service Safety Laundry Maintenance (bldgs., equipment) To promote activity for the achievement of rehabilitation goals consistent with the client's ability to profit. To assist with placement of the client when maximum rehabilitation has been achieved.	To provide for safety needs and maintenance needs as client's hip heals. To provide Rehabilitation Therapy consistent with return to normal ambulation ff. hip fracture. To locate someone to provide the necessary help at home to provide for her needs ff. healing of the fracture, rehab therapy and discharge.	To maintain muscle strength. To help client learn transfer and ambulation skills consistent with nonweightbearing (L) leg. To promote independence and self-esteem. To provide safety. To promote preservation of joint mobility (L) hip. To provide social and occupational therapies consistent with client's individual needs and motivation.	To require the client to perform those activities of daily living within her capabilities. To give required assistance to client in activities of daily living. To reinforce learning of transfer skills. To promote independence and self-esteem. To assist in provision for social needs. To assist with provision of maintenance needs and safety requirements. To promote healing of the decubitus.

FIGURE 5. PROVIDER GOALS FOR CARE OF MS. C. (A PORTION OF THE MEANS STANDARD)

Outcomes of care. The identification of specific expected outcomes of care may or may not be possible at the outset of planning. Clients whose response to care cannot be predicted in the initial phases of planning for care include those with flaccid hemiplegia from stroke, the chord-injured client with quadriplegia, the client with multiple sclerosis, the client with rheumatoid arthritis, and others.

For Ms. C. it was possible, on the basis of her history and present condition, to predict specific expected outcomes—some immediately and others as soon as assessment by the team had occurred. (See Figure 6.) The predictions in the two columns on the right in Figure 6 represent the maximal ends standard for Ms. C. at a particular time. (Means standards or ends standards are subject to change.)

In nursing outcome, a behavioral norm for Ms. C. had to be identified before measurable outcome criteria were set. (See Figure 6, last column, item no. 4) For example, on July 25, 1974, after several days of observation, the following was recorded:

Ms. C. is calm, cooperative, alert; oriented to time, place and person; complains reluctantly; is impatient occasionally, reacts with anger to appropriate stimuli; is forgetful of some recent events; is pleasant and interacts easily and comfortably with personnel and others; states that she is satisfied with her present maintenance and therapy and understands the need for these, but wishes she could be at home.

On the basis of this observation, item no. 4 might be restated in more specific terms. (See Figure 6, last column, item no. 4.)

The Nursing Home—Expected Outcomes	The Nursing Home—Expected Outcomes for Ms. C.	Multidisciplinary—Expected Outcomes for Ms. C.	Nursing—Expected Outcomes for Ms. C.
The maintenance needs of nursing home clients will be provided for. Rehabilitation activities and therapies will be provided consistent with client's ability to profit. Satisfactory placement and arrangements will be secured for those patients whose maximum level of rehabilitation has been reached.	The client will suffer no accident or injury during her stay in the nursing home. The client will receive maintenance care consistent with her basic needs and pathophysiological problems. The client will receive rehabilitation therapy designed to maintain hip joint mobility and return the patient to normal ambulation. The client will return to her home with appropriate assistance personnel to provide for her needs there.	Muscle strength will be maintained sufficient to allow the client to ambulate and give self-care. The client will learn to transfer safely from bed to wheelchair and wheelchair to commode. The mobility of the (L) hip joint will be preserved at a functional level. The client will demonstrate the highest level of independence in self-care and ambulation of which she is capable (allowing for non-weight-bearing requirements during stay and at discharge). The client will receive supportive care and social function therapy consistent with demonstrated behavior and expressed needs.	The client will: (1) Perform activities of daily living independently, except for assistance with: washing back and legs putting on stockings fastening back fasteners on clothing transfer from bed to wheelchair and wheelchair to commode grooming of hair and nails (2) Demonstrate safe transfers with assistance ff. teaching regarding non weight-bearing transfer. (3) Suffer no injury or accident attributable to care by nurses. (4) Demonstrate verbal and nonverbal behavior suggesting satisfactory adjustment to the environment and therapy provided. (5) Achieve complete healing of the decubitus in the sacral area by day of discharge.

FIGURE 6.   EXPECTED OUTCOMES OF CARE FOR MS. C. (ENDS STANDARDS)

Problem	Action
(1) Unable to perform all of hygienic care and dressing activities: Unable to reach back and legs for washing and dressing purposes. Unable to fasten back ties and buttons. Requires assistance with grooming of hair and nails.	(1) Provide assistance in activities of daily living. Wash back and legs. Assist to put on stockings. Assist to tie back ties or fasten buttons. Assist to fasten hair in place after combing. Cut and file nails as needed.
(2) Drinks less than 2,400 ccs per day.	(2) Force fluids to 2,400 ccs daily and record.
(3) Bowel movements do not occur at regular times, therefore require special treatment and scheduling.	(3) Record bowel elimination daily and establish routine for same. Encourage client to eat a high roughage diet.
(4) Does not know how to effect safe, nonweight-bearing transfers. Forgets to lock wheelchair.	(4) Teach, reinforce, and supervise nonweight-bearing transfers from bed to wheelchair and wheelchair to commode. Elicit verbal feedback about transfer procedure and safety precautions frequently.
(5) Partially deaf—no hearing aid. Communication is difficult.	(5) Speak loudly and clearly to client and elicit verbal feedback often.

The client will retain her usual behavior patterns (as described on 7/25/74) and demonstrate no emotional responses such as crying, screaming, tantrums, resistance, depression, withdrawal, or pathological mental states during her treatment period (i.e., the period between admission and discharge).

It should be noted that making specific predictions about the emotional responses of clients is at present a rather risky business. All individuals go through stages of adjustment that include regressive behavior and idiosyncratic use of defense mechanisms, all of which may fall within the definition of "normal" behavior but which could represent deviation from "usual" behavior. Disagreement about the meaning and/or interpretation of behavior, plus the variables of time and availability of resources, etc. are only some of the factors that may influence or negate prediction of and/or accomplishment of behavioral outcomes. Much work remains to be done in this area.

The means standard. The planning process proceeds from (1) the identification of broad/specific aims and outcomes for each problem listed in the nursing diagnosis to (2) decision making about the nursing action required. An example of the action portion of the means standard for Ms. C. for problems listed in Figure 4 under Maintenance Needs is shown above.

The action standard above represents a *maximal* standard of nursing care for the selected problems listed. Any omissions in the above standard could bring the plan below a safe level and would be likely to have a negative effect on preventive and restorative outcomes. However, standards can be manipulated and often are. In terms of priority, actions 1, 2, and 4 are top-level; if circumstances required it, actions 3 and 5 might be omitted temporarily. An absolute safe minimal standard of care (short-term) could then be said to be comprised of actions 1, 2, and 4. In addition to defining the standard, manipulating the standard is an important responsibility of the professional nurse.

Exploration of the effect of several variables on standards for nursing care are beyond the scope of this article, but are available in the literature. However, we will identify several of the more crucial variables affecting the means standard. These are:

(a) The value orientations of the client and family.

(b) Resources available to accomplish the means standard.

(c) Value orientations of the involved health care providers.

(d) The decision process and the value of the various alternative actions on solution of the patient's problems.

(e) The consensus on standards obtainable among the multiple members of the group of health care providers.

(f) The health care requirements of the whole group of clients in the environment.

(g) The interrelationships between certain problems, actions and outcomes for the individual client.

Enforcement of standards. Both ethically and legally, the enforcement of standards for nursing care is a function of the professional nurse. It is a function for which she is held accountable no matter what responsibilities she may delegate to others. The nursing care plan she devises is dynamic, constantly subjected to the changes that evolve from the eco-system, from execution of activities within the plan, and from pressures exerted by extraneous forces. The nurse must have information about these changes. Moreover, she must know whether the actions identified were carried out and whether the expected outcomes of client care are being achieved (or whether movement continues toward achievement of the broad means objective).

Quality control. For the nurse to obtain the information necessary for accountability, an operational feedback system is required[3]. A plan for quality control activity is established prior to the execution of the nursing care plan. The nursing action standard (means standard) as well as the control (feedback) plan must be determined with due consideration of the whole group of clients being served and the resources available to provide service and obtain feedback.

Feedback methods. A variety of methods to obtain feedback may be used, including the following:

1. Observation of client, environment, and ongoing activity.
2. Verbal exchange with the client.
3. Verbal feedback from the nursing staff.
4. Examination of records written by nursing staff.
5. Multidisciplinary conferences with physician, occupational therapist, physical therapist, etc.
6. Reading progress notes of physician and other therapists.
7. Informal feedback from other health care providers, visitors, and/or agency personnel.
8. Solicitation of expert opinion.
9. Maintenance of a written Nursing Care Plan on Kardex (or other).
10. Other methods appropriate to the setting and situation.

The example provided is the control activity identified to obtain feedback on execution of the means standard for Ms. C.

Control Program:

8:00 a.m.   Observe client as she performs hygienic care and grooming. Elicit verbal feedback regarding activities of daily living.

9:00 a.m.   Observe transfer from bed to wheel chair, checking for nonweight-bearing on (L) leg, locking of wheelchair, position of wheelchair for transfer.

11:00 a.m.   Check Intake Record.

Feedback Data—Means Standard

First day post planning

8 a.m.　Client has necessary equipment and clothing—is bathing self and reports nursing assistant and will wash back and legs and assist with dress.

9. a.m.　Nursing assistant placed wheelchair, and gave step-by-step instructions to client while nonweight-bearing transfer was accomplished safely. Client strength was adequate for safety. Giving instructions difficult due to client's partial deafness.

11 a.m.　Intake record shows 600cc.

2 p.m.　Nursing assistant reports client performed all activities of daily living as planned; resists drinking fluid (intake only 900cc); bowels have not moved—this recorded; ate all food including greens for lunch; used bedpan at bedside (no time to take to bathroom); grumbles about not going to bathroom—no other complaints or notable behaviors.

Conclusions re: Means Standard
(1) Minimal Safe Standard met.

(2) All other standards met except verbal feedback on transfer and fluid intake too low for this hour.

Control Action Decision:

Plan with evening staff for forcing of 1300cc fluid between 3 and 9 PM

Evaluation Decisions:

Means standard acceptable and will not be changed.

Feedback Data—Ends Standard

First day post planning

Client is performing all activities of daily living related to hygienic care, grooming, and dressing.

Client accomplished safe nonweight-bearing transfer safely with maximum assistance.

Verbal feedback on transfer procedure not elicited.

Client selected wearing apparel, juice offered at 10 AM, and use of free time in-AM. She did not get to use commode for elimination as preferred.

Intake level lower than should be at 2 PM. Likelihood of accomplishment standard reduced.

Some discontent because unable to go to bathroom.

Conclusions re: Ends Standard
Standards No. 1, 2, and 3 met at acceptable level.

No. 4 met, with exception of verbal expression of dissatisfaction (not serious).

Control Action Decision:

None today—Continue daily observation

Evaluation Decisions:

Ends standard achievements are within acceptable limits—No change needed.

FIGURE 7.　DATA OBTAINED FROM IMPLEMENTATION OF THE
CONTROL PROGRAM RELATED TO PROBLEMS LISTED FOR MS. C.

2:00 p.m. Elicit verbal feedback from Nursing Assistant in regard to Ms. Cheeter's bowel elimination, total fluid intake, transfer activity, independence in activities of daily living, attitudes, and behaviors.

Nursing Execution

Implementing controls. Implementation of the control program occurs concurrently with the execution of the nursing care plan.* Feedback data obtained through the control program is used during execution of the nursing care plan to prevent the occurence of drastic or unsafe deviations from the predetermined standard. These data are used as the basis for action decisions to return the means standard to its predetermined level. They are pooled with feed-in data, all of which must be considered throughout the execution phase and evaluation phase of the nursing process to determine whether either or both the means or ends standards should be changed. An example of feedback related to both means and ends standards is presented in Figure 7.

Nursing Care Evaluation

Evaluation of the nursing care of a client or group is a process through which a determination is made whether the care was appropriate, acceptable, and effective or not. As a result of this activity, a decision will be made whether or not to revise the plan, and if so, the nursing process begins a new cycle through a new action plan and standard for care.

Evaluation process. The nurse is concerned with all available feedback from her control program. She collects this (Phase A,

---

*Execution, a part of the nursing process, is the implementation of the nursing action identified in the nursing care plan, and the maintenance of (at least) a minimum safe standard of nursing care for the client.

Figure 8) and examines it to see if the standards set for both means and ends have been achieved (Phase B). If it is too soon to expect an observable outcome, she may be able to use the absence of negative outcomes, or a "no change" outcome, to judge the status of the ends standard. For example, if an expected outcome for Ms. C. is "complete healing of the sacral decubitus by day of discharge," the nurse may not see a definitely observable change in one day's time. She observes the decubitus and may conclude that there is "no change" because she sees neither formation of new granulation tissue or negative signs. She establishes through feedback whether the means standard has been achieved, and acts to correct the standard achievement if it falls below a safe minimal level (Phase E). She may sometimes go directly from consideration of omissions in the means standards (Phase A) to Phase C, where she decides the care is not appropriate, and then to Phase D, where she decides on corrective action (change in the means standard), and finally to Phase E, or implementation of the action.

If, for whatever reason, expected outcomes are not stated the broad goal (means standard) assumes a most important role in keeping care directed toward an "ideal" ends standard which may or may not be realistic/achievable for a particular client.

SUMMARY

Nursing process is a series of dynamic interrelated activities carried out to fulfill the purposes of nursing. Nursing process is composed of both direct care activities (execution) and indirect care activities (assessment, diagnosis, planning, evaluation) aimed at producing outcomes for the client which are accountable in relation to quality and quantity. It is a logical, rational approach to nurse activity for client-centered care.

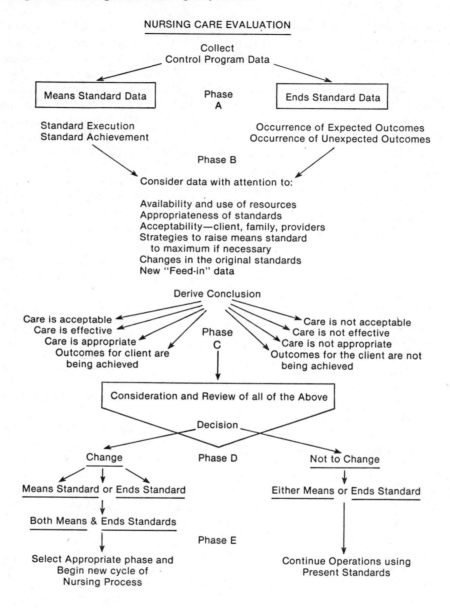

FIGURE 8. THE FIVE PHASES OF EVALUATION IN NURSING PROCESS

Quality control programs are devised and carried out concurrently with the execution of the nursing care plan. These provide the nurse with data needed to maintain at least a minimal safe standard of nursing care throughout the client's continuum of care. Quality control is essential to quality assurance.

REFERENCES

1. Murchison, I.A. and Nicholls, T.S. *Legal Foundations of Nursing Practice.* New York: Macmillan, 1970, pp. 90, 470.

2. Murchison, I.A. and Nicholls, T.S., 1970.
3. Nicholls, M. Quality control and patient care. *Am. J. Nurs.*, Vol. 74, No. 3, 1974, p. 457.

BIBLIOGRAPHY

American Nurses' Association. *Standards of Nursing Practice.* Kansas City: American Nurses' Association, 1973.

Bircher, A. On the development and classification of diagnoses. *Nurs. Forum*, Vol. 14, No. 1, 1975, pp. 10–29.

Bloch, D. Evaluation of nursing care in terms of process and outcome. *Nurs. Research*, Vol. 24, No. 4, 1975, pp. 256–263, July-August, 1975.

_____ Some crucial terms in nursing—what do they really mean? *Nurs. Outlook*, Vol. 22, No. 6, 1974, pp. 689–693.

Carrieri, U.K. and Sitzman, J., Components of the nursing process. *Nurs. Clinics North Am.*, Vol. 6, No. 1, 1971, pp. 115–124.

Durand, M. and Prince, R. Nursing diagnosis: process and decision. *Nurs. Forum*, Vol. 4, 1966, pp. 50–64.

Giblin, E., ed. Symposium on Assessment as Part of the Nursing Process, *Nurs. Clinics North Am.*, Vol. 6, No. 1, 1971, pp. 113–209.

Little, D. and Carnevali, D. *Nursing Care Planning.* Philadelphia: J.B. Lippincott, 1969.

Mundinger, M. and Janson, G. Developing a nursing diagnosis. *Nurs. Outlook*, Vol. 23, No. 2, 1975, pp. 94–98.

Ryan, B. J. Nursing care planning: a systems approach to developing criteria for planning and evaluation. *J. Nurs. Admin.*, Vol. 3, No. 3, 1973, pp. 50–58.

Stevens, B. Analysis of trends in nursing care management. *J. Nurs. Admin.*, Vol. 2, No. 6, 1972, p. 12.

Yura, H. and Walsh, M. *The Nursing Process.* New York: Appleton Century-Crofts, 1973.

Chapter 13

Health Care Outcomes: Who Did What?

Virginia G. Wessells
Ann F. Klein

The multidisciplinary approach to treatment of clients with a variety of diseases and disabilities has been used for a number of years. The most persistent and visible multidisciplinary groups have practiced in units or agencies where rehabilitation is the major focus of care. Interdisciplinary input has been accomplished through preadmission screening of the client, and through joint planning sessions that identify problems, determine objectives, select action to achieve the objectives, and evaluate the outcomes. These groups have had varying degrees of success in rehabilitating their clients over the years, and they have gradually become more proficient in execution of the process. There is, however, considerable work to be done in (1) identifying realistic expected outcomes (setting ends standards) for the client, and (2) showing that the input of any one discipline was essential to achievement of the outcome. These are two important issues that must be addressed, for the whole group as well as the individual disciplines are being pressured to give evidence of accountability in practice.

This chapter will examine some of the difficulties encountered by interdisciplinary care providers in formulating expected outcomes, and in particular, the difficulty in demonstrating that the input of any one discipline was essential to the successful achievement of the outcome. The authors will illustrate the problems through use of a sample case treated in their practice in a rehabilitation nursing home facility.

The staff of the nursing home included the disciplines of medicine, nursing, pharmacy, physical therapy, occupational therapy, social service, and dietetics. There were also consultation services available from specialists within those disciplines, and from other disciplines (dentist, psychiatrist, respiratory therapist, etc.). The interdisciplinary staff met weekly to discuss clients on a scheduled basis. In addition, there was formal and informal interaction both in and out of meetings that helped produce collaborative agreements in regard to each client's care.

PATIENT HISTORY

The client for discussion is Mrs. M., a thirty-four-year-old white woman with a ten-year history of rheumatoid arthritis. She was admitted to the nursing home for treatment of a pressure ulcer on the left leg that occurred as a result of application of a cast to the leg for immobilization and healing following synovectomy of the left knee. She was hospitalized for an extended period and then sent home to complete the healing process. This wound, however, enlarged, became infected, and would not heal. The wound was incised, drained, and sutured, but subsequently dehisced a second time. Mrs. M. was pursuaded to accept admittance to the nursing home because the rheumatoid arthritis was in acute exacerbation and because it appeared that she needed a protected environment in which to achieve healing of the wound. Concurrent diagnoses on admission were pernicious anemia and monilia vaginitis.

Mrs. M. is a small, attractive woman with pale skin and dark curly hair, which she wears shoulder length. She has a moon face and the bland expression of the client on cortisone therapy. She is a divorcee whose two girls live with her in a low-cost housing development. The third child, a boy, lives with the father. The client's income and medical care costs are derived from Medicare, Medicaid, and Aid to Dependent Children funds. The local Welfare Department furnished a housekeeper five days a week to stay with the girls during Mrs. M.'s stay at the nursing home. At night and on weekends, the girls stayed with church friends and relatives both in and out of the city. Mrs. M. was quite concerned about her children and kept in touch daily by phone.

Mrs. M. has a history of noncompliance in relation to use of muscles and joints when her disease was in acute exacerbation. As a result, she now has severely limited range of motion in the ankles, cock-up toes, limited finger flexion with ulnar drift, and hyperextension of the middle-phalangeal joints. Both elbows were overstretched and painful.

She could not actively flex them and obtained a functional range of motion by substitution with shoulder and scapular motion. Supination and pronation of the arm were very limited and wrist motion almost nonexistent. Instead of normal use of a cane for ambulating, she walked by fixing her arms close to her trunk and leaning her trunk onto the cane for weight bearing. She required help to complete dressing activities, and at times could not comb her hair because of pain in the shoulders. She jerked herself into a standing position by rocking and using mainly hip flexor muscles to stand. She could not propel a wheelchair due to her upper extremity involvement.

Mrs. M. completed high school prior to her marriage and her intelligence was assumed to be average. She was however, euphoric, hypertalkative, and unrealistic about use of time and her own responsibility for execution of therapeutic regimens. Her conversation and response to questions suggested that she might have little insight into the negative effects of her past noncompliance with rheumatoid arthritis regimens.

The arthritic drug therapy used preadmission was continued during her treatment at the nursing home:

Solganol (Gold) 50 mg, once a month (I.M.)
Enteric Coated Aspirin 3 tablets, 4 times a day
Prednisone 1 mg, 3 times a day
Valium 5 mg, 3 times a day

Other drugs ordered were:

Diethylstilbestrol 0.5 mg, once a day (25 times per month)
Santyl Ointment to leg ulcer once a day
Vitamin B-12 100 mg (I.M.) once a month
Betadine Douche for Monilia infection, once a day for 7 days

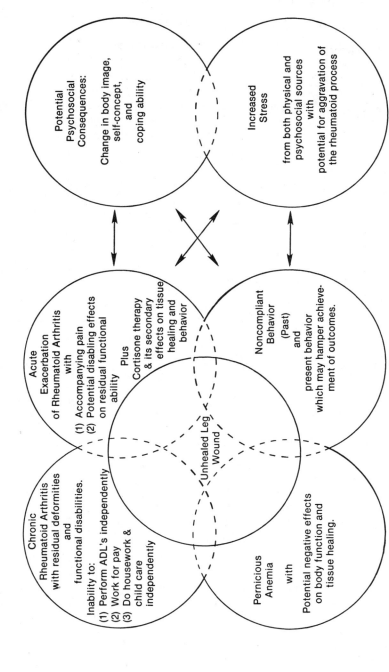

FIGURE 1.   THE INTERLOCKING PROBLEMS THAT AFFECT THE SETTING OF BOTH MEANS AND ENDS STANDARDS (FOR MRS. M.)

Physical therapy orders were:

Whirlpool to left leg 10–15 minutes, once a day, 5 times weekly

Hydrogen Peroxide Spray to leg wound as necessary

Santyl Debridement of leg wound daily

Reston around wound followed by application of bulky dressing

Myoflex pack to painful joints 5 times weekly

Arthritic exercises, 3 to 5 repetitions to all extremities every day

Ambulation in parallel bars with 4-point gait every day

CARE OBJECTIVES

Mrs. M.'s problems were overlapping and interlocking. (See Figure 1). Because of the effects or possible effects of each problem area on various other problem areas, the team concluded that a maximum means standard, which includes all possible actions for all problems, must be devised and executed. This standard would include actions to:

(1) Promote healing of the leg wound.
(2) Reduce the inflammatory process in the joints to preserve joint function and provide comfort.
(3) Maintain range of joint motion and muscle strength.
(4) Improve ambulation ability.
(5) Decrease stress to lowest possible level.
(6) Promote client adaptation to changing body image and to maintain self-esteem.
(7) Assist the client to cope with institutional restraints and therapeutic regimens.
(8) Promote the highest level of independent function possible.
(9) Encourage compliant behaviors to therapeutic regimens.

Psychosocial Care

Since all areas of care for Mrs. M. had equal priority, the selection of objectives 5 through 9 for initial discussion in this chapter is an arbitrary one. In these care areas, the providers had the least expertise in identifying specific behavioral objectives and outcomes, and therefore, worked toward broad and vaguely identified outcomes. Moreover, there was no concerted attempt to use behavior modification techniques. The group did identify actions aimed at preserving body image, self-esteem, and coping ability while containing stress-anxiety factors at the lowest possible level. For example, each discipline planned time arrangements carefully to give the client enough time to do all of the self-care possible, and then required that she do it. Members of the various disciplines were involved in setting limits on Mrs. M.'s noncompliant behaviors as well as encouraging and rewarding her positive behaviors.

Nursing and Social Service were instrumental in obtaining a telephone for the client to keep at her bedside to talk daily with the housekeeper, thus allowing her involvement in home and child care management. The clinical nurse specialist conferred daily with the client and acted as liaison and coordinator between disciplines to promote therapeutic environment. The physician ordered weekend passes for home visits on several occasions.

The Social Service and Occupational Therapy Departments were involved in diversional-functional activities as a means of improving Mrs. M.'s morale and maintaining body image. Weekly interdisciplinary conferences provided an opportunity for feedback, and promoted sharing and planning for management of the psychosocial environment.

The evaluation of the psychosocial care of Mrs. M. in this agency was deterred by factors commonly found in health care agencies. The care providers had low access to such specialists as a psychologist or psychiatric-mental health specialist and themselves had limited expertise in identifying realistic behavioral outcomes, so they identified none. They had limited knowledge of behavior modification techniques and their use, and therefore did not really attempt to change Mrs. M.'s attitudes and behaviors. They did agree that evaluation of achievement of the objectives would be determined by (1) whether the actions decided upon were actually executed, and (2) whether the client continued to comply with planned regimens.

Evaluation

We will always wonder what might have happened had we been working for more specific outcomes. We do know that Mrs. M. complied reluctantly with some aspects and willingly with other aspects of the regimen, and that the actions planned to achieve the psychosocial objectives were carried out most of the time.

All disciplines contributed to achievement of the means objectives 5 through 9. Each discipline could show through data collection that the client did "comply with the recommended regimens" concerning that discipline, and that they had carried out the actions decided upon to achieve the outcomes. However, for lack of specific outcomes stated in behavioral terms, no discipline could show that it actually achieved "decrease of stress levels to lowest possible levels" or "client adaptation to changing body image and self-concept."

The psychosocial areas of care are problematic for defining expected outcomes of care, and the expertise of behavioral specialists if required to assist with these definitions. Lack of such input reduces the quality of the standard of care (means and ends) and often deprives the whole group of providers from identifying what effect their input had on outcomes.

Physical Care

Physical care problems are more specific and observable. In this case, treatment of the unhealed leg wound demonstrates the nature of interdisciplinary care, and furnishes data for discussion of the difficulty likely to be experienced if one discipline wishes to show that its input is crucial to the achievement of expected outcome. This problem is shown diagrammed in Figure 2, with both means and ends standards identified.

In Figure 2, the center circle lists the primary problem (leg wound) as well as concomitant problems affecting wound healing. The middle ring identifies the means standard for each discipline, and the outer ring the ends standards. Each discipline has a slice of the pie with input essential to achievement of the final outcome: "The wound of the left leg will heal competently."

The major thrusts in wound healing focused on nutritional intake, reduction of leg and wound edema, and cleansing and debridement of the wound. Nursing and Dietetics share a means standard: ("Maintain optimal nutritional intake for wound healing") and an ends standard ("The client will eat one-half or more of each serving of food on her tray at each meal"). Medicine writes the diet order for High Protein Diet. Dietary plans the menus, prepares and serves the food, without which Nursing could not contribute its particular action, which is: to prepare the food tray, cut meat, and open cartons (essential to eating for this client because of her physical inability to do those three things). Who shall get the credit for achievement of the objective? It is possible that all of us may be frustrated in reaching the goal because the client may refuse to eat the food.

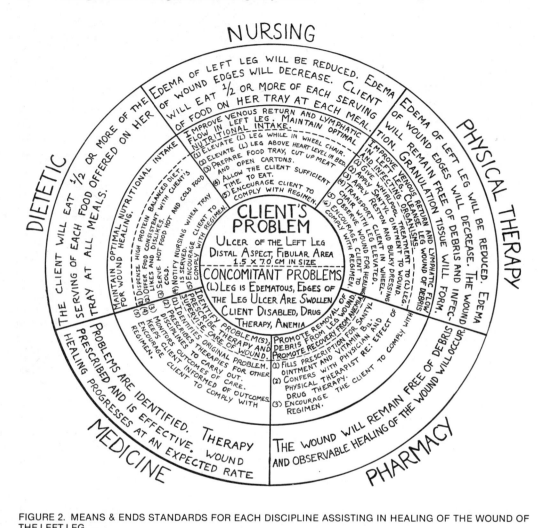

FIGURE 2. MEANS & ENDS STANDARDS FOR EACH DISCIPLINE ASSISTING IN HEALING OF THE WOUND OF THE LEFT LEG

Actually, the client consistently ate very well and with little urging from anyone. In terms of achievement of the means standard, there were many problems, e.g., keeping food hot, getting nursing personnel to prepare the tray and food, and permitting the client time to eat. In the final analysis, Dietary, Nursing, and the client all played crucial roles in meeting the ends standard. The contributions of the three appear inseparable. There is no measure available to assess the effect of dietary intake on achievement of the final expected outcome ("The wound will heal competently")—this can only be assumed.

Nursing and Physical Therapy shared ends standards ("Edema of the left leg will be reduced" and "Edema of the wound edges will decrease"). Who can say whether whirlpool and pressure dressings were the most important means, or whether the elevation of the leg in the wheelchair and bed were the crucial treatments?

Evaluation revealed that the client's non-compliant behavior often got in the way of goal achievement. Constant vigilance on the part of nursing personnel, in particular, was required to get the client to lie down and elevate the leg as ordered during the day. She did comply with this requirement at night and while riding in the wheelchair. She went home on pass on two weekends and returned with the leg very swollen each time. She admitted that she had not done as she was asked to do at home—keep the leg elevated above heart level at least 50 percent of the time.

The physician diagnosed Mrs. M.'s leg wound and prescribed therapy: whirlpool to left leg; clean wound with hydrogen peroxide spray and apply Santyl ointment for debridement followed by protective bulky dressing. Two other disciplines are involved in this action—Pharmacy and Physical Therapy. All three are essential. The physician is the only one who has the legal authority and expertise to diagnose and prescribe therapy. His input is crucial, in that no one else can do those particular activities. Pharmacy fills the prescription—an action only the pharmacist is permitted to do. The Physical Therapist plans and executes the treatments, and it is hoped the client will comply with the regimen. The input of the client and of all providers are crucial to the outcome.

In the final outcome, Mrs. M. was discharged from the Nursing Home wearing a Unna paste boot and Elastoplast dressing from the left foot (excluding toes) to knee to maintain the competence of the healed wound. She returned as an outpatient for several weeks to have the boot removed, wound examined, and the boot reapplied. Eight weeks after treatment was begun, the physician decided that "The wound of the left leg was competently healed" and all treatment of the wound at the Nursing Home was discontinued. Objective 1 was achieved.

This brings us to objectives 2, 3, and 4, which relate to arthritis treatment and maintenance of physical functional ability. Figure 3 illustrates input (means standard) from the five disciplines involved, and from the patient-family as well. The action standard for Mrs. M. (Figure 3, upper right) is one passively agreed to by her.

For this group of objectives, it can be seen that Medicine, Nursing, and Physical Therapy contributed action to achieve all three, while Occupational Therapy contributed to the achievement of two and Pharmacy to one. The specific means standard for Nursing was: (1) administer drug therapy as prescribed (Solganol); (2) allow and require the client to take her oral medications at the bedside (no small ritual!); (3) plan and execute personal care, feeding, and toileting regimens to allow the client time to participate to a maximum in her own care; (4) encourage the client to walk and exercise her joints at intervals during periods of low activity. Actions 1 and 2 may have played an important role in the achievement of an "idealistic" ends standard. ("The joint inflammation will be reduced"). Since such a standard is nonmeasurable as well as somewhat idealistic, Nursing must be content with knowing that the actions identified were carried out.

All disciplines were severely confined in relation to objective 2, since the outcomes of care were highly dependent upon these variables:

(1) The effectiveness of the particular drug as treatment to reduce inflammation
(2) The client's particular physiological response to the drugs

Means Objectives:

No. 2. Reduce the inflammatory process in the joints→preserve joint function and provide comfort.

No. 3. Maintain range of joint motion and muscle strength→retain ability to carry out activities of daily living.

No. 4. Improve ambulation ability.

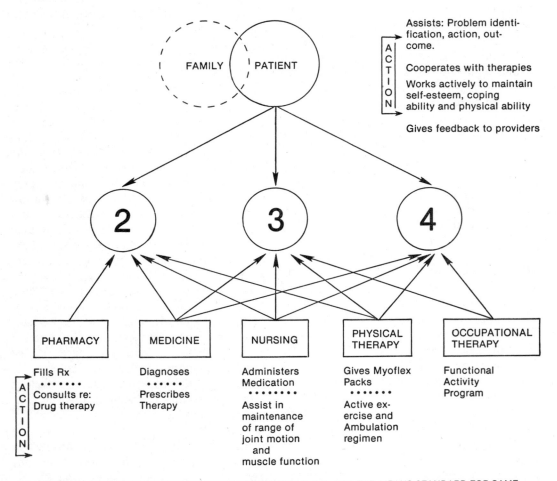

FIGURE 3.   INTERDISCIPLINARY INPUT INTO OBJECTIVES 2, 3, 4, AND THE MEANS STANDARD FOR SAME

(3) Whether the drugs were given by Nursing as ordered

(4) Whether Physical Therapy regimen was carried out and was effective

(5) Whether the client complied with the regimens

The difficulty of predicting outcomes was increased because of the particular joints that were inflamed. For example, a measurable statement of outcomes for the elbow, knee, wrist, and ankle joints could be: "The joint swelling will be reduced," as determined by measurement of joint size with a centimeter tape before and after treatment. But since the hip joint, shoulder, hand, finger, foot, and toe joints, cannot be measured by tape, a more subjective and relatively nonmeasurable standard must be set: "The joint will become less painful," as identified by verbal statement by verbal statement from the client that "The joint is less painful during movement."

Again, for objective 3, prediction of expected outcome would be risky with Mrs. M. To the variables mentioned above for objective 2 could be added:

Length of time postsurgery (for the knee joint).
Lack of exercise and movement due to the inflammation and pain.
Patient's toleration for stress of the arthritic exercises.
Danger of reducing range of motion as a result of malalignment of the joint.

In fact, maintenance of present range of motion could not be predicted with assurance. For example, the physical therapist took goniometer measurement of the following joints at admission and found:

Left knee range of motion: 10 to 93 degrees flexion (Normal: 0 to 125–130)
Right shoulder range of motion: 90 degrees flexion (Normal: 180 degrees)
Right elbow range of motion: 0 range (passive motion) to 130 degrees active motion (Normal: 0 to 145–160) (using compensatory shoulder and trunk action).

Active motion was inhibited in some of these because of inflammation, but was improved by physical therapy treatments (heat, Myoflex Cream). As a result, the client was able to perform the arthritic exercises. A combination of drugs and physical therapy, including injection of Cortisone into the right shoulder joint, was instru-

mental in changing the range of motion from 90 degrees to 135 degrees.

At the conclusion of treatment, motion had been maintained in all joints, motion in the left knee had improved from 0 to 93 degrees and in the right shoulder to 135 degrees flexion.

Testing for muscle strength was not done with Mrs. M., but could have been used as a means of establishing status on admission, with testing again at conclusion of treatment to show that muscle strength had been maintained. Instead, gross functional ability was used as a measurement.

Objective 4 was not achieved, despite Physical Therapy treatments and walking in parallel bars. Mrs. M. continued walking with a waddling gait, using the cane as previously.

As we considered the data, it seemed to us that no one discipline could claim that its input was responsible for any outcome identified. We also concluded that the client should have been a more active participant in selecting goals and the actions to achieve them. By and large, the providers imposed their goals on Mrs. M. and she played the role of passive accepter. We need to study the role of the client in the decision-making process and in the formulation of outcomes. Mrs. M. is a good example of a client who had seriously damaged her functional ability because she chose not to comply with her treatment regimens in the past. For purposes of standard setting, all providers should consider including the client in decision making, and should study the results. The questions need to be asked—will the outcomes achieved have a lasting effect and will they contribute to the client's long-term goals?

Quality assurance regulations will soon require that all care providers produce data to show that their input did indeed produce outcomes for the recipient of care. There seems little doubt that each discipline will have to show that its input contributed to specific outcomes, but there is much doubt that any individual discipline can claim that its input alone was responsible for most outcomes. Thus, we are faced with a long struggle to become expert at role negotiation. This will be especially difficult since we are all neophytes at defining *realistic* expected outcomes!

To expand a bit on this problem: to date, each discipline has viewed itself as a separate entity with a unique function. This has tended to promote a jealous guarding of function and has worked negatively for role negotiation. We still guard our function and will continue to do so as long as we have identity as individual disciplines. However, when we involve ourselves in "Health Care," we join a group that includes the client and his family. The group works toward "ideal outcomes" and formulates realistic expected outcomes as quickly as possible, based on study of the variables involved (existing condition/situation, potential for change, barriers to change, and resources available). Since more than one discipline (along with the client) has responsibility for most outcomes, shared outcomes must be made more acceptable to health care providers as well as to clients.

BIBLIOGRAPHY

Donabedian, A. *A Guide to Medical Care Administration,* Vol. II American Public Health Association, 1969.

Harvey, A.M. et al. (eds.). *The Principles and Practices of Medicine,* 18th ed. New York: Appleton-Century-Crofts, 1972.

Leonard, B. J. Body image changes in chronic illness. *Nurs. Clinics N. Amer.,* Vol. 7, No. 4, 1972, pp. 687–695.

Levin, T. *American Health: Professional Privilege vs. Public Need.* New York: Praeger, 1974.

McDonald, F.J. and Harms, M.T. A theoretical model for a nursing curriculum. *Nurs. Outlook,* Vol. 8, 1966, pp. 48–51.

Moidel, H.C. et al. *Nursing Care of the Patient with Medical-Surgical Disorders.* New York: McGraw-Hill, 1971.

Moore, M.L. The measurement of joint motion, Parts I & II. *Phys. Therapy Rev.,* Vol. 29, 1949, pp. 256–264, 195–205.

Murray, R.L.E. Body image development in adulthood. *Nurs. Clinics N. Amer.,* Vol. 7, No. 4, 1972, pp. 617–629.

Physician's Desk Reference. New Jersey: Medical Economics Company, 1974.

Ramey, I.G. Setting nursing standards and evaluating care. *J. Nurs. Admin.,* Vol. 3, 1973, pp. 27–35.

Robinson, C.H. *Normal and Therapeutic Nutrition.* New York: Macmillan, 1972.

Zimmer, M.J. "Quality Assurance for Nursing Care", from *Conference Proceedings, Quality Assurance for Nursing Care,* American Nurses' Association, 1974.

UNIT IV
CASE STUDIES

Introduction

The chapters in this unit are from authors representing a range of specialty areas in nursing. They include practitioners and teachers in Mental Health, Community Health, Pediatric, Geriatric, and Acute Care Nursing. All were asked to review a fairly typical patient's care and to examine the manner in which standards were set, to identify factors that might or did influence the standards, and to determine the degree of achievement of the standards. They were encouraged to recommend solutions.

Only two constraints were placed on the contributing authors—(1) the focus must be on standards rather than on nursing process alone, and (2) the studies and discussion should be reality-based. As a result, several approaches are used and more than one viewpoint expressed.

Auterino and Hogan set means and ends standards for an acutely ill patient with myocardial infarction. They identify the methodology used by the nurse to obtain feedback for control purposes and they compare the expected outcome with the actual outcome.

Beeker and Kimball focus on an adolescent with a traumatic injury and present selected examples of evaluation of goal achievement. They stress the importance of identifying factors that interfere with goal achievement in order to obtain direction for future decision making.

Bullock describes the adoption and adaptation of problem-oriented recording in the facility where she is employed. She presents a case study that includes a plan of nursing care involving the setting of standards (ends) with defined time limits. She gives examples of S.O.A.P. notes and shows how outcomes are evaluated and recorded.

Hanner and Nicholls identify means and ends standards for a client in a community health setting and compare projected and actual outcomes of care. They conclude their chapter by identifying some factors that deter standard setting in community nursing.

Chapter 14

Application of Standards in Critical Care Nursing

Georgia Autorino
Mary E. Hogan

Accountability is receiving increased attention in both the general and the professional literature. We call for accountability in government, in education, and in the professions. When applied to nursing, accountability means the need to justify nursing practices. By virtue of licensure, registered nurses are legally accountable for the nursing services provided to clients.

Accountability requires continuous evaluation of two general aspects of nursing practice: (1) performance, and (2) the effect of performance upon the health status of the client served. In order to be valid and reliable, evaluation must be based upon specific outcome criteria. Standards for practice have been defined by the profession. These standards must be brought to the arena of direct care and be refined by each nurse in relation to each client served. Identification of outcome objectives (or ends standards) for each individual patient gives us this refinement. Those nursing practices by which ends standards are achieved are called means standards. Quality control is the process whereby practice is measured against standards and action taken to maintain the standards.

One of the most widely voiced criticisms of health care delivery in this country is that the consumer, locked in by his lack of specialized knowledge relating to the practice of medicine, and unable to judge the quality of his health care, cannot afford to obtain a second expert opinion because of the exorbitant costs involved. The lay person has very few avenues of recourse to assure himself that the care he receives is up to the current level of practice. The rising number of malpractice suits reflects an attempt to challenge the quality of care delivered.

To date, there have been few commonly accepted standards that were known by both the consumer and provider of health care. The creation and dissemination of standards of health care will give both the consumer and the provider a means of identifying quality care. It provides the consumer with knowledge of the basic levels of quality care and, with this, a certain level of quality can be assured. It aids the health care provider by giving tools to measure his/her performance and the outcomes of that performance against established levels. This measurement could be made by individual providers, by departments, or by a committee for quality assurance comprised of various levels of providers and consumers.

The purpose of this case study is (1) to demonstrate how standards and quality control of nursing care are applied in an acute clinical setting, and (2) to illustrate the dynamic nature of the planning and quality control process. Coronary care has become an accepted area of specialized clinical nursing. Coronary care nursing was one of the first areas in which the role of the nurse was expanded and in which documented evidence has been collected demonstrating nursing's effectiveness in saving lives and improving the quality and productivity of the lives that were saved [1,2]. The nurse's role includes the use of comprehensive assessment skills (such as arrhythmia identification, physical assessment, and interpretation of laboratory tests), and the responsibility for carrying out therapeutic measures which include delegated medical functions. The nurse's actions are based on defined protocols set by the medical staff in collaboration with nursing service and hospital administration. A case study involving the planning of care for a person with an acute myocardial infarction has been selected for discussion.

After a summary clinical presentation, we will attempt to assess the immediate nursing problems, establish ends standards (objectives), define means standards (plan of care), identify information feedback necessary to determine whether the standards were met, and demonstrate dynamic evaluation and adjustment of care for a person in the early phase of recovery from a myocardial infarction. We will also show how available resources influence the application of this process and will identify what modifications in standards might be necessary.

CASE STUDY

J.B., a fifty five-year-old male, was admitted to the coronary care unit of the local community hospital with the diagnosis of possible myocardial infarction (M.I.). He had awakened at 4:00 a.m. unable to catch his breath and suffering severe, crushing substernal pain radiating to his left arm and shoulder. The CCU nurse observed an alert, pale, diaphoretic, and anxious-appearing person. Vital signs were : T-99.8 (oral), P-58 (radial and apical), R-24 and B.P. 100/60. His skin felt cool and his hair was wet with perspiration. Distended neck veins were not perceived, and veins of the hands were flat in the neutral position. Recognizing the need for pain medicine, the nurse questioned him about allergy and he denied any. The patient verbalized concern about his condition by asking, "What is happening to me?"

Assessment is the first step in the nursing process. It is based on data, including subjective symptoms, objective observations made by the nurse, laboratory reports, and a knowledge base. After a rapid initial assessment was carried out and an M.I. was assumed to have occurred, the following immediate problems were identified.

1. Danger of lethal arrhythmia
2. Pain
3. Difficulty breathing
4. Anxiety
5. Danger of pump failure, congestive heart failure of cardiogenic shock

Often, in CCUs, nurses accept responsibility for carrying out defined protocols*and nursing routines without clearly identifying ends standards (specific objectives) in relation to patient problems. The effectiveness of such protocols and routines is rarely evaluated in terms of achievement of ends standards. Instead, effectiveness of care is evaluated in terms of what was done for the patient. (This brings to mind the old

---

*The authors use the term *protocols* to mean actions defined by legitimate authority as opposed to routines that come into being as the result of everyday performance or custom.

saying, "The treatment was successful, but the patient died.") If nurses are to be accountable, assessment must include identification of ends standards, and evaluation must determine whether the ends standards were achieved. This is the foundation upon which quality assurance is built. Quality control involves obtaining data necessary to determine if the ends and means standards are met, and quality assurance becomes the proof that the standards were met.

From the above problems, we have identified objectives that should be achieved within the first few hours, and these become our ends standards:

Problem

1. Danger of lethal arrythmia
2. Pain
3. Difficulty breathing
4. Anxiety
5. Danger of pump failure, congestive heart failure or cardiogenic shock

Ends Standards

1. The patient will not develop a lethal arrhythmia.
2. The patient will indicate relief of pain.
3. The patient will indicate ease in breathing.
4. The patient's anxiety will be relieved.
5. The patient will not develop pump failure.

According to Nicholls, ends standards must meet three criteria. They must be understandable, achievable, and measurable [3]. In this case, the defined objectives are deemed understandable on the basis of the knowledge and frames of reference common to nurses working in coronary care areas. Achievability of some defined objectives depends on certain variables over which there is no human control. There may be high risks within the patient himself—such as overall physical condition, previous cardiac status, general circulatory status, or concomitant disease or disability—and despite the use of comprehensive physiological monitoring and the institution of all available preventive and therapeutic measures, lethal arrhythmia and/or pump failure may develop. At this point in this patient's care, nursing lacks information that might give ends standards more specificity in relation to achievability and understandability. As more information is received, objectives can be revised.

There exists statistical correlation between such factors as location of infarct, history of previous ischemia, age of patient, presence of intraventricular conduction defects, heart size, degree of lung congestion, admission systolic blood pressure, and the eventual outcome for the patient [4]. Prediction of outcomes based upon such factors can help us formulate more achievable objectives. We feel that the objectives relating to arrhythmia and pump failure are justifiable, as they are based upon data collected on morbidity and mortality for such patients. In the precoronary care unit era, arrhythmias accounted for 47 percent of deaths due to M.I. while ventricular failure accounted for 43 percent. At present, lethal arrhythmia accounts for only 1 percent of the deaths due to M.I. This drastic decrease in deaths is attributed to the early recognition and treatment of warning arrhythmias. The major problem that still exists is ventricular failure. Overt left ventricular failure occurs in about 60 percent of patients with M.I. and is the cause of death in 93 percent of patients dying after M.I. This death rate could be decreased if incipient or preclinical left ventricular failure were detected and treated [5].

The achievement of objectives 1, 2, 3, and 5 is measurable, as we will demonstrate in discussion of information feedback. Objective 4 is not measurable. The condition of anxiety is assumed to exist, for it is the usual reaction of an individual to a life-threatening situation; the patient's question about what was happening to him did indicate anxiety. Further assessment is required to verify and clarify the problem. This standard (the relief of anxiety) lacks a tool for measurement appropriate to the acute care setting. Research should be done on the definition and measurement of nursing standards related to relieving anxiety in such settings.

From the identification of problems and ends standards, the plan of care can be derived. This plan of care becomes the means standards, and it incorporates the protocols and regimens prescribed by other members of the health care team. To control the process, and thus assure quality care, information feedback systems must be established and maintained. To do this, it is necessary to simply identify ways for the nurse to determine whether ends and means standards are being met. For example, the ends standard, "The patient will not develop a lethal arrhythmia," requires information about the patient's heart rhythm. The most direct source of this information is the cardiac monitor.

Other less direct sources are vital signs and observations indicative of cerebral functioning. The information necessary to determine if the means standard was met involves checking to see that the nursing staff did, in fact, carry out the prescribed plan. In the case under study, let us consider the objectives, plan, and information feedback.

PROBLEM 1. DANGER OF LETHAL ARRHYTHMIA

Ends Standard

The patient will not develop a lethal arrhythmia.

Feedback for Ends Standard. Did the patient develop a lethal arrhythmia? Nursing action to ascertain feedback: attach patient to a cardiac monitor.

Means Standard

1. Control ectopic pacemakers:
   a. Start IV and maintain at keep-open rate
   b. Give lidocaine 100 mg IV bolus for PVCs prn followed by lidocaine drip of 1–4 mg minute to control PVCs.
   c. Control pain and anxiety. See plan for objectives 2 and 4.
   d. Defibrillate immediately with 400 watt-seconds for ventricular fibrillation.

2. Control conduction defects:
   a. Report any observations of conduction defect immediately to physician.
   b. Teach patient to avoid straining to prevent valsalva effects.

3. Maintain heart rate between 60–100/ minute:
   a. Control bradyarrhythmias by:
      1. Administration of Atropine 0.5 mg IV for heart rate of 50 or less.
      2. Check heart rate before administering morphine for pain.
   b. Control tachyarrhythmias by:
      1. Limiting activity to bedrest with possible commode privileges.
      2. Avoiding exciting stimuli.
      3 Controlling pain and anxiety.
      4. Notifying physician of heart rate above 100/minute.

Feedback for Means Standard. Was the plan carried out by the staff? Monitor quality of staff performance based on stated means standards through direct observation and/or audit of records.

PROBLEM 2. PAIN

Ends Standard

The patient will indicate the relief of pain.

Feedback for Ends Standard. Did the patient verbalize pain relief? Were nonverbal signs indicative of relief? Nursing action to obtain feedback: ask patient and observe patient for restful appearance or sleep.

Means Standard

1. Morphine 10 mg IM stat and q3–4 hours prn.
2. Provide comfort measures. See plan for Problem 3.
3. Give O_2 at 2–4L/minute nasal cannula to reduce ischemia.
4. Keep open IV for use as a rapid route for analgesia.

Feedback for Means Standard. Were the nursing measures carried out by the staff? Monitor through observation and through check of records.

PROBLEM 3. DIFFICULTY BREATHING

Ends Standard

The patient will indicate ease in breathing.

Feedback for Ends Standard. Did the patient verbalize ease in breathing? Were nonverbal signs indicative of ease in breathing? Nursing action to obtain feedback: ask the patient, assess patient's respiratory rate and pattern, observe nares for flaring, chest for retractions, observe skin color and nail beds, and patient's activity.

Means Standard

1. Give O_2 at 2–4 L/minute by nasal cannula.
2. Position in semifowlers to high fowlers to promote lowering of diaphragm.
3. Loosen restrictive clothing.
4. Use pillows to support back.
5. Tell patient to take long, slow, deep breaths.

Feedback for Means Standard. Were the prescribed nursing measures carried out? Monitor nursing performance.

PROBLEM 4. ANXIETY

Ends Standard.

The patient's anxiety will be relieved.

Feedback for Ends Standard. Was the patient's anxiety relieved? Nursing action to obtain feedback: observe for sweating, increase in heart rate, restlessness, facial and verbal expressions of anxiety. Because of the lack of an appropriate tool to measure this standard, evaluation is subjective.

Means Standard

1. Using simple terms, tell patient why he is in the unit, what the health team is doing to and for him—repeat often. Answer questions.
2. Assign nurse to remain with patient throughout admission and until condition is stabilized.
3. Control pain and difficulty in breathing. See plan for objectives 2 and 3.
4. Allow brief visit with wife to allay fears for wife's well-being.
5. Ask patient if he has any immediate concerns that you can assist him with, for example, notifying his place of business that he is in the hospital.
6. Valium 5 mg p. o., t.i.d. (as prescribed by physician).

Feedback for Means Standard. Were the prescribed measures carried out? Monitor nursing activities and records.

PROBLEM 5. DANGER OF PUMP FAILURE —CONGESTIVE HEART FAILURE OR CARDIOGENIC SHOCK.

Ends Standard

The patient will not develop pump failure.

Feedback for Ends Standard. Did the patient develop signs of pump failure? Nursing action to obtain feedback: check chest x-ray for signs of interstitial edema indicating early phases of heart failure.

Listen to chest sounds for the presence of rales. Auscultate heart for splitting of sounds and the presence of rales. Auscultate heart for splitting of sounds and the presence of extra heart sounds. Observe neck veins for distention and venous pulsations. Observe for the development of cyanosis. Check extremities for venous engorgement and dependent edema. Check abdomen for palpable liver or ascites. Measure fluid intake and urine output. Monitor cerebral function. Frequent checks of vital signs.

Means Standard

1. Initiate a limitation of fluid intake to 1500 cc.
2. Order a 2 gm sodium diet.
3. Notify physician of any detected signs of heart failure.
4. Detect and terminate arrhythmias. See plan for Problem 1.
5. Since pain causes a sympathetic response, give morphine liberally—as per plan for Problem 2.

   Feedback for Means Standard. Did the staff carry out the prescribed measures? For example, check intake and output sheets and diet tray, as well as chart.

When defining standards for quality assurance, one must consider the availability of the resources necessary to maintain them. The configuration of physical, mechanical, and human resources available has a significant influence on the setting of standards and their maintenance. This patient was admitted to a special unit, and it can be assumed that the mechanical and human resources needed to carry out the means standards and achieve the ends standards were available. If he had been admitted to a small hospital lacking the facilities of a coronary care unit, the above care plan could not have been carried out. Even if the aforementioned facility, with trained coro-

nary care nurses, some of the prescribed measures might not be appropriate under certain circumstances. In larger medical centers, such procedures as pulmonary wedge pressure, pulmonary artery pressure, cardiac output measurements, echocardiography, and phonocardiography might be part of the total monitoring regimen for detecting physiological derangements that can lead to pump failure. This would require significant modification of the prescribed standard.

The final phase of the process of quality control involves the use of feedback to evaluate achievement of ends and means standards, and to determine the effectiveness of the means standards in meeting the ends standards.

EVALUATION

Ends Standard 1. The patient will not develop a lethal arrhythmia. The standard was met.

Means Standard. No ectopic pacemaker was observed. Pain and anxiety were controlled (see evaluation for ends standards 2 and 4). A conduction defect was noted. The monitored defect showed first-degree A-V block with a P-R interval of .28 seconds. The heart rate was not maintained between 60–100/minute initially. At one point atropine .5 mg was administered IV and the heart rate increased to 64/minute with a P-R interval of .20. The patient was maintained on bed rest and was allowed to rest in between treatments and necessary monitoring. The means standard regarding patient teaching to avoid straining was deemed inappropriate because the patient, in the first few hours, was too anxious to participate in a teaching-learning process. All but one means standard was met. Means standards were effective in meeting the ends standards as tested thus far. Testing will be continued. Patient teaching regarding the avoidance of straining was postponed.

Ends Standard 2. The patient will indicate relief of pain. Within the first half hour, J. B. verbalized relief of crushing pain, but stated that he still had a heaviness in his chest. Within one hour, he verbalized complete relief.

Means Standard. Morphine sulfate 10 mg was administered IM short after the patient's arrival in the unit. After 30 minutes, 2 mg was given IV. Heart rate at this time was 60/minute. The patient was positioned in semifowlers for comfort. Oxygen was started by nasal cannula at 4 L/minute. The patency of a vein was maintained with 5 percent dextrose and water at 30 cc per hour. The patient was given morphine 10 mg but still complained of pain. The ends standard of pain relief was not reached because the means standard (morphine 10 mg IM) was not effective. After 30 minutes, the means standard was revised and 2 mg morphine sulfate was given IV. All means standards were met. Revised, they were deemed effective in meeting the ends standards.

Ends Standard 3. The patient will indicate ease in breathing. The patient verbalized ease in breathing within 30 minutes. He stated that the oxygen helped him. Respiratory rate decreased to 18/minute. Color improved. The ends standard was met.

Means Standard. Oxygen was administered at 4 L/minute. Patient was positioned in semifowlers. Clothing was loosened but not removed until the patient verbalized relief of pain and dyspnea. The patient was instructed to take slow deep breaths through his nose in order to receive maximum benefit from the oxygen. All means standards were met. They were effective and will be continued for 24 hours.

Ends Standard 4. The patient's anxiety will be relieved. The patient verbalized neither the presence nor the absence of anxiety. He quietly accepted treatment and nodded in response to the nurse's communications. After the pain was relieved his facial expression appeared quiet. Due to lack of appropriate feedback, we could not evaluate the achievement of this standard. At this point, achievement of this standard can only be presumed if the plan is carried out.

Means Standard. All means standards were met, with the exception of number 6. Valium was not given in the first hour. It will be started. We could not ascertain the effectiveness of the means standard because we could not measure the ends standard.

Ends Standard 5. The patient will not develop pump failure. The patient did not develop signs of pump failure. Thus, the standard was met insofar as we could assess the clinical picture. Chest x-ray had not been done. Chest sounds were clear to auscultation. Auscultation of the heart revealed a normal two-sound sequence with a soft first heart sound. Decreased intensity of S1 could be due to congestive heart failure; to myocardial infarction itself, which causes a reduction in force and velocity of ventricular contraction; or to a delay in A-V conduction[6]. When the abnormality was perceived, the patient's P-R interval was .28 seconds. After the administration of atropine, the first heart sound seemed as loud as the second heart sound. The soft first heart sound was therefore attibuted to the delay in A-V conduction. No gallop sounds, murmurs, or rubs were heard. Neck veins were undistended at 45 degree head elevation. and venous pulsations were absent. There was no venous engorgement or edema of the extremities. Palpation of the abdomen had not been carried out; the abdomen did not appear distended. The patient had not voided. He remained alert and oriented, remembering events leading to admission.

Means Standard. Within the first hour, the patient was given 30 cc of 5 percent dextrose and water IV. No diet was started. The physician was notified of the observed heart sound changes; no treatment was ordered. Bradyarrhythmia and first degree A-V block were detected and treated (see evaluation for ends standard 1). Pain was relieved (see evaluation for ends standard 2). All means standards were initiated. The assessment of their effectiveness in meeting the ends standard requires continuation of the plan.

The above summary of events taking place within the first few hours following J. B.'s admission to the coronary unit is only a summary. Certainly, other events occur during the first hours after admission. An EKG would be done. Blood would be drawn for complete blood count, enzymes, routine chemistries, and blood gas analysis. Chest x-ray would be done. Emergencies would be handled as they arose. A complete history and physical examination would be carried out by the physician. The nurse would perform more comprehensive assessment of the physical and psychosocial status of the patient. All of these activities contribute more data and require modification of the initially indentified standard.

The authors agree that the formalization of this process requires much time and thought from the nursing staff, and that the extensive process described in this chapter might be impractical in the acute clinical setting. However, once the process has been written up, it is possible to formulate standard care plans for patients with myocardial infarction. The standards identified in this chapter apply to most patients entering the hospital with a possible myocardial infarction. Certainly, relieving pain, preventing lethal arrythmias, and decreasing anxiety are universal goals in caring for heart attack victims. Now these goals can become standards of care and a basis for which levels of performance can be identified and evaluated. The plans then need only be modified for differences in specific client's needs—as this plan was modified when the means standard providing for morphine 10 mg IM failed to relieve pain and the standard was revised to give 2 additional mg IV with more successful results. An abbreviated flow sheet can be used to give direction to action and to act as a tool to collect feedback data.

It is our contention that unless (1) specific outcome standards are identified in the assessment phase of the nursing process, (2) means standards are thoughtfully planned and implemented, and (3) ongoing evaluation carried out, nurses will find it difficult to justify the practices to which they subscribe.

Inadequate documentation of planned nursing intervention makes it difficult to validate quality assurance in nursing. The nursing care plan is not part of the client's legal record. This leads to lack of communication concerning the effectiveness, partial effectiveness, or ineffectiveness of nursing interventions. If an intervention is found to be unsuccessful or only partially successful, what assurance is there that at some future date nurses will not waste their time and the client's investment by attempting such intervention again? Physicians orders are part of the legal record. Why then are not nursing plans? We propose that all nursing care plans be incorporated into the client's legal record, as nursing orders and progress toward goals be documented and retained in the nurses notes.

Another problem related to quality assurance is that the lines of authority as well as the responsibility for implementing nursing plans are often muddled and ineffective. In many clinical settings, nurses on different shifts may not carry out interventions defined by other nurses. There must be some person who has the responsibility for seeing that the nursing care plan is carried out. This person must have authority, given to her by nursing service. Ideally it would seem that the head nurse is that person.

To assure quality care for clients, the nursing service administrator must be responsible for determining the effectiveness of her nursing staff. In the past, the nursing service administrator was concerned with covering clinical areas that had a specified number of patients—the number determined by some remote efficiency expert who based his estimate on a task analysis. The administrator's time was spent looking into accident reports, collecting data on the number of patients who died, sending down directives and communications from above, and investigating patient and family complaints. It was a rare nurse administrator who looked into the average patient's problems—unless

he died, received the wrong medication, fell out of bed, or his family complained about the care he received. If nursing is going to be responsible for the delivery of quality health care, nursing service administrators must look into goals and objectives for the average client and monitor the effectiveness of care via nursing audit and peer review programs. Where deficiencies and inconsistencies exist, administrators must lead and develop their staff so that they can resolve such problems. This can be accomplished by increasing staff in problem areas; providing inservice programs on goal setting, evaluation and quality assurance; improving orientation programs; and utilizing such resources as the clinical specialist nurse researcher or nurse epidemiologist.

Nurses are responsible for their actions. If any action cannot be explained in terms of what it is accomplishing for the client, then it has no place in the practice of nursing. It is time that nursing separated the empirical from the scientific.

REFERENCES

1. Meltzer, L. E. "Current Concepts of the Coronary Care Unit," in *Lectures in Cardiology, a Listener's Notebook.* S. E. Moolton, (ed.), Philadelphia: The Charles Press, 1972, p. 60.
2. Abdellah, F. G. The physician-nurse team approach to coronary care. *Nurs. Clinics N. Am.,* Vol. 7, No. 3, (1972), p. 428.
3. Nicholls, M. E. Quality control in patient care. *Am. J. Nurs.,* Vol. 74, No. 3, 1973, p. 458.
4. Mulligan, C. D. Continuing evaluation of coronary care. *Heart and Lung,* Vol. 4, No 2. 1975, pp. 227–231.
5. Meltzer, L. E., 1972, pp. 59–65.
6. Martin, F. and Alvarez-Mena, C. *Cardiovascular Physical Diagnosis.* Chicago: Year Book Medical Publishers, Inc., 1973.

Chapter 15

Evaluation of Goal Achievement in the Care of an Adolescent with a Traumatic Injury

Barbara Ann Beeker
Linda Stevenson Kimball

A major goal in pediatric nursing is to assist the child and his family to cope with the stresses that accompany an illness. While we realize that the biophysical and psychosocial self are interrelated, our primary focus in this presentation will be on the psychosocial needs of an adolescent with a traumatic injury.

CASE STUDY

Bob L., a fourteen-year-old boy, was brought into the emergency room at 1 p.m. on a Saturday by his parents, who stated their son's left arm had gotten caught in a hay bailer. In addition to his obvious traumatic crushing injury, x-rays revealed a fractured humerus. He was taken to the operating room for revascularization surgery. Although able to save the arm, the surgeon could not predict the extent to which the patient would regain use of it.

Data Base

The nurse's initial assessment data was obtained from the parents. She learned that the family is composed of six members: Mr. and Mrs. L., and four children, aged 17, 15, 14, and 8. They are of German origin and belong to the Lutheran Church.

The family lives on a dairy farm where, according to Mr. L., "Everyone is expected to do their share of the hard work." The patient was a healthy child except for a brief hospitalization at age three for pneumonia. Currently in the ninth grade, he is an average student but excels in mathematics, which is his favorite subject. Mrs. L. volunteered that Bob is active in school sports and was looking forward to playing basketball this year. She described him as an outgoing boy who relates easily to most people. She also mentioned that he is left-handed.

While caring for Bob the nurse added the following information to her data base:

1. The patient spends much of his time staring out the window or at the ceiling.
2. His communication with the staff is primarily limited to answering yes or no to questions asked of him.
3. He does not ask for help in activities that require the use of two hands. For example, if the nurse forgets to cut his meat, he leaves it untouched and says he isn't hungry.

4. He gets very angry when he is awakened twice each night for his dressing change.
5. He complains about bedtime restrictions and the early hour that he is awakened in the morning.
6. He appears bored and lonely. When asked what he would like to do, he states, "nothing."

7. He continually asks his parents if they think he will be able to make the basketball team this year.

Nursing Diagnoses and Goals

On the basis of the data obtained, the following nursing diagnoses were made and corresponding goals formulated for Bob's care.

Nursing Diagnosis	Goal
1. Patient is anxious about the outcome of his injury.	1. Patient will be able to deal with his anxiety to the extent that: a. he will verbalize his fears. b. he will recognize those fears which are not reality-based. c. he will focus on other things than his injury.
2. Patient is in the depression phase of the grieving process.	2. Patient will progress through the grieving process to the extent that he will be able to accept that he may have limited use of his arm.
3. Patient is having difficulty coping with the limitations placed on his activities as a result of his injury.	3. Patient will make plans that include a. alternate ways to accomplish his activities of daily living. b. alternatives to being on the basketball team. c. alternatives to using his left hand for writing. d. alternate ways to share in the farm work.
4. Patient has temporarily lost his usual peer support system.	4. During hospitalization, patient will develop and maintain an alternate peer support system.
5. Patient is concerned that his hospitalization has limited his ability to make decisions he is accustomed to making on his own.	5. Patient will make as many decisions as possible within the limits of hospital policy and his condition.
6. Normal family living patterns have been disrupted as a result of his illness.	6. The family will modify their current living patterns to the extent that: a. the mother will not spend an inordinate amount of time at the hospital. b. the needs of the other family members are not neglected. c. essential household and farm chores are accomplished.

Evaluation

The remainder of this chapter will deal with evaluating the achievement of goals 1 and 4, which are of primary significance to the adolescent because: (1) an adolescent's sense of security and self-worth is derived from acceptance by his peer group, and (2) an important developmental task for the adolescent is deciding on the vocation he will follow as an adult. The loss of function that this patient may experience can limit his range of choices in planning for his future. Such a deforming injury poses a threat to the adolescent's body image, and he fears rejection by his peers.

Goal 1. To meet this goal, the nurse planned to observe the patient for verbal and nonverbal signs of anxiety and to determine what he knew about his injury and its possible outcomes. She also planned to provide him with opportunities to express himself, and to give him accurate and consistent information at his level of understanding. In addition, she would determine what his outside interests were so that when he was ready to focus on other things, she would be able to provide diversional activities.

Early evidence that Bob was moving toward achievement of goal 1 (able to deal with his anxiety) occurred on day four of his hospitalization. Although dressings had been changed every six hours around the clock since admission, this was the first time that Bob was able to bring himself to look at his arm. His immediate response was to grimace and turn his head away. This response was followed by, "What's all that black stuff? My arm looks pretty bad, doesn't it?" When the nurse told him that his arm appeared to be healing, he did not seem convinced—as evidenced by his comment, "You're probably just saying that." At each subsequent dressing change, he carefully inspected his arm and asked,

"Does it look any better?" When the nurse reflected his question and asked him if he thought it looked any better, he responded, "I'm asking you." The nurse then reassured him that she really did think it looked better, but that the healing process was slow and that he couldn't expect to see progress overnight.

On day six, when the nurse returned from her days off and sat down purposefully to talk with Bob, he was able to ask, "Do you think my arm will always look this bad?" As a result of the nurse's consistent efforts to help him express his fears, she learned that his primary fears at this time were whether or not he would have full use of his arm and whether he might still lose his arm due to an infection. Since the nurse knew that at this point loss of his arm was an unrealistic fear, she asked him what made him think he was going to lose it due to an infection. He stated that he overheard the doctor talking to his mother about the danger of infection and that his mother had said she hoped that he would not lose his arm.

When questioned further, Bob said he had overheard this conversation the day after he had been admitted. The nurse helped him look at the facts (that he was on antibiotics to prevent infection, and that the time when infection usually occurred had now passed). She suggested that he might want to discuss the problem with the doctor. His response was, "Oh, no. I don't want him to know how dumb I was to think that."

The nurse received one of her first clues that Bob was perhaps ready to focus on things other than himself when she overheard him ask his parents if anyone from school had called about him. Because the nurse was aware that his attention span was likely to be short in this initial passive period, she provided him with such diversions as television, radio, and sports magazines. Initially, he would tire of a television program midway through the show, but by the end of the second week of hospitalization, he could focus on a TV program to the extent that he would respond to the nurse's discussion of the program. The nurse helped him move toward activities that required his active involvement by suggesting that he ask his mother to get him a book on mathematical puzzles or brain teasers.

Goal 4. The nurse's plan of action in relation to this goal included (1) identifying individuals who could serve as the patient's alternative support system and (2) providing opportunities for him to interact with them.

Although parents, teachers, and other adults are less important to the adolescent than his peer group, the adolescent does tend to regress in a time of stress and depend initially on his parents for support. Early in his hospitalization, Bob very much depended on his parents—as evidenced by his unwillingness to have them leave when visiting hours were over. His mother spent many long hours at his bedside because she felt that he needed her. During this initial period, Bob did not establish any relationship with his thirteen-year-old roommate. He was too involved with himself and his injury to care that another boy shared his room, and the roommate was discharged on Bob's third hospital day. As his progress continued, dependence on his mother as his primary support system decreased. Initially he allowed her to leave his room only for a short break; later he could tolerate the fact that her visits with him were shortened because of all the catching up she had to do at home.

The nurse tried to identify possible age-mates who might serve as a support system for Bob since his roommate had been discharged. Two other adolescent boys, ages fourteen and fifteen were sharing a room on the floor. On Bob's ninth hospital day, when one of these boys was discharged, he was moved to the room with the remaining boy and introduced to his new roommate, age fifteen. Initially, the two boys were cautious with each other, each testing out the possibility of acceptance by the other. It looked as if they would provide each other with the needed peer support system. However, their developing relationship was suddenly interrupted when, two evenings later, the other boy's condition took a turn for the worse, and he was transferred to the pediatric intensive care unit. In the nurse's judgment, there were no other patients at this time who might be able to serve as an alternative peer support system.

At the end of the second week of hospitalization, goal 4 (Bob would develop and maintain an alternative peer support system) was not achieved. Even though the goal had not been achieved, the nurse felt it had been a realistic one, since the usual adolescent census on the pediatric unit is six. Therefore, the probability that the patient would be the only adolescent on the unit was low.

Because the necessary resources, that is, age-mates, were not available, the nurse revised the goal to be: the patient will re-establish his usual peer support system. Although the nurse felt this goal was now appropriate in terms of patient and agency resources, she felt that it would not have been appropriate earlier in his hospitalization. At that time, he was on bedrest with his arm constantly elevated, and he could not participate in such goal-directed activities as using the pay telephone in the hall to talk to his school friends or visiting with them in the coffee shop.

SUMMARY

In addition to determining whether patient goals were met, the nurse must identify those factors that supported and those that interfered with goal achievement, so that she can make decisions regarding future actions.

One factor that initially interfered with meeting goal 1 was the fact that not all the staff were equally adept at recognizing verbal and nonverbal signs of anxiety. Thus, many early signs were missed. Other negative factors affecting the achievement of this goal were (1) inadequate staffing during the patient's hospitalization, and (2) the technical complexity of the physical care required by his arm, demanding most of the staff's attention and time. An important factor supporting achievement of the goal was the organization of nursing care in the form of primary nursing care, which assured the patient of contact with the same "primary" nurse over his period of hospitalization. Further support was provided by group participation in a staff conference to develop plans to help Bob express and deal with his fears.

Initially, there were two factors that supported achievement of goal 4. First, the nurse was able to help the mother recognize when it was appropriate for her to readjust her priorities, and second, the nurse was able to support him in his beginning relationship with a new roommate. Despite the initial progress toward this goal, the subsequent absence of any age-mates on the pediatric unit negated any possibility of goal achievement.

The care a patient receives is influenced by such factors as the experience and education of the staff, the patient-staff ratio, and the degree of flexibility within the institution. The professional nurse must take all these factors into consideration when deciding what goals she can realistically expect to achieve in caring for a given patient.

CONCLUSION

This case study was presented to demonstrate that the quality of nursing care can be evaluated in terms of goal achievement. When one considers that this presentation dealt with only a small portion of the totality of one patient's care, one realizes the complexity of implementing an evaluation system. However, in order to improve patient care, nurses can and must accept their professional responsibility to evaluate goal achievement.

BIBLIOGRAPHY

Daniel, W. A. Jr. An approach to the adolescent patient. *Med. Clin. North Am.*, Vol. 59, 1975, p. 1281.

Dempsey, M.O. The development of body image in the adolescent. *Nurs. Clin. North Am.*, Vol. 7, 1972, p. 609.

Fujita, M.T. The impact of illness or surgery on the body image of the child. *Nurs. Clin. North Am.*, Vol. 7, 1972, p. 641.

Nicholls, M. Quality control in patient care. *Am. J. Nurs.*, Vol. 74, 1974, p. 456.

Riddle, I. Nursing intervention to promote body image integrity in children. *Nurs. Clin. North Am.*, Vol. 7, 1972, p. 651.

Chapter 16

The Promotion of Quality Assurance through Problem-Oriented Recording

Nancy Repass Bullock

Many nurses have found problem-oriented recording to be an excellent vehicle for documentation of the quality of care given to patients and families. Problem-oriented recording has been adapted in various settings[1, 2, 3].

The nursing staff of the Richmond City Health Department initiated an adaptation of problem-oriented recording in 1974. They adopted a defined data base, complete problem list, plans for the problem, and progress notes in S.O.A.P. format. With this plan, they wanted to promote family-centered nursing care and continuous evaluation of nursing care. Consistent with their family emphasis, data bases were developed for both patient and family. Behavioral objectives were written for each problem identified on the problem list in the beginning of the process. During evaluation, a date is placed in the result column when the objective is achieved.

The S.O.A.P. format for progress notes (as used in the basic problem-oriented recording system) was adapted as follows:

The term *Assessment* was replaced with the term *Action*. The staff's rationale for the change was that Assessment (in their definition) was included in the (S)*Subjective* and (O)*Objective* part of the S.O.A.P. format and in the statement of the problem. The term *Action* (A) was defined to mean action taken by anyone to alleviate the problem. (P)*Plan* included both immediate and future plans. The rationale was that the (A)*Action* section required a description of the activities that occurred during contact with the patient and/or family, a necessary component of documentation of nursing care. The (P)*Plan* section would describe both immediate and future methods of achieving objectives with the family. The following case study illustrates how the Richmond City Health Department adapted problem-oriented recording.

CASE STUDY

While reviewing a maternity and infant referral from a public health nurse coordinator at a local hospital, the public health nurse discovered that Frances Parsons (fictitious name), a twenty-one-year-old white female, had a low forceps delivery on

December 4, 1974, followed by a urinary tract infection. Medications prescribed for her were Gantrisin and birth control pills. She had a six-weeks checkup appointment at a Family Planning Clinic at the health department on January 17, 1975.

The newborn infant, Kathy had a grade-two systolic ejection murmur in the pulmonary area. Kathy had been referred to the state health department's program for handicapped children, the Bureau of Crippled Children. She had an appointment on January 3, 1975, at its Cardiology Clinic. The infant also had a six-weeks checkup appointment at a Pediatric Clinic at the health department on January 15, 1975.

The public health nurse made her first home visit to the family on December 12, 1974. Utilizing the Richmond City Health Department's problem-oriented family record, she collected assessment information on the family roster, family data base, and the patient data bases for the mother and infant (Table 1).

From this assessment (Table 1) and the mother's patient data base, the public health nurse noted the problems that she and the family identified on the problem list.

TABLE 1. FAMILY DATA BASE

FF Name: Parsons

LONG-RANGE GOAL: Family copes with activities of daily living
and seeks help when needed by 12/76.

DATE	SOCIOECONOMIC:
12/12/74	Earl (husband) has seasonal employment as sheet rocker for Ball Construction Co. making $160./wk. Family has no knowledge of urban resources and no relatives living in Richmond. Earl has 10th grade education.
	ENVIRONMENT:
12/12/74	Moved from Henderson, N.C. 11/74 (rural area); live in one-bedroom second-floor apt. in transient neighborhood. Hot and cold water; steam radiator heat; and small kitchen with gas stove. Apt. clean but cluttered. Furniture worn but adequate; Frances states that apt. has roaches. (PHN did not observe.)
	FAMILY RELATIONSHIPS:
12/12/74	Frances cares for infant with help of Earl and her mother, who is visiting temporarily. Earl is supportive to Frances.
	ATTITUDE AND COPING ABILITY:
12/12/74	Earl (23 years old) and Frances have been married two years. Both are willing to seek solutions to problems, but need help with complicated tasks (using urban resources; understanding medical diagnosis)

Table 1 (continued) PATIENT DATA BASE

PATIENT'S NAME: Kathy   FAMILY NAME: Parsons

LONG-RANGE GOALS: 3/13/75 Kathy performs developmental tasks according to age and physical limitations and follows medical supervision by 12/76.

DATE	CHIEF COMPLAINT:
12/12/74	Grade-two systolic ejection murmur in pulmonary area. No other cardiac symptoms; under BCC.
	PRESENT ILLNESS: (from infant referral)
12/12/74	Heart murmur detected on newborn exam.
	PHYSICAL EXAM:
12/12/74	TPR: 99.6-120-34 Body posture: good Birth wt.: 6 lbs. 2 oz. Reflexes: all normal Present wt.: 6 lbs. 2 oz. Navel healing Fontanels: non-bulging No shortness of breath, Color: rosy cyanosis, or irritability. Muscle tone: good Elimination: adequate Spontaneous movement: good
	NUTRITIONAL STATUS:
12/12/74	Similac with iron 4 oz. six times daily. Aseptic sterilization method.
	PAST HISTORY:
12/12/74	ILLNESSES: Heart murmur HOSPITALIZATIONS: MCV North 12/4/74 - 12/7/74 INJURIES: None OPERATIONS: None MEDICATIONS: None BIRTH HISTORY: Low forceps delivery, Apgar 5-7-9; 40 wks. gestation. Birth wt.: 6 lbs. 2 oz.; PKU done. ALLERGIES: None
	PSYCHOLOGICAL STATUS:
12/12/74	Parents have adequate supplies for infant and seem capable of caring for her. See mother's Patient Data Base
	REHABILITATION-VOCATIONAL POTENTIAL:

PROBLEM-ORIENTED RECORDING

According to the *Problem-Oriented Recording Orientation Manual* of the Richmond City Health Department, a *problem* is "any condition, situation, concern or need in which a patient or family requires help to attain or maintain physical, mental, or social balance"[4]. Problems are categorized according to four basic areas of concern: sociological, psychological, demographic, and medical.

The Problem List

Each problem is assigned a number which is not used again for another problem. Therefore, throughout the record, problem number 1 would always be the same problem. The problem list consists of all patient and/or family problems that have been identified (Table 2). Problems are listed whenever there are sufficient data in the record to justify listing them. Prior to inscribing a problem on the list, the nurse writes the name of the patient or family to which it pertains above the problem number and title. The date beside the problem title refers to the date at which the problem was first identified by the public health nurse[5].

Objectives

During the planning phase of her nursing care, the public health nurse wrote one or more behavioral objectives for each problem identified. According to the *Problem-Oriented Recording Orientation Manual*, a behavioral objective is "the mutually agreed upon behavior that demonstrates the desired result of the nurses' involvement with the patient and/or family"[6]. The objective is written in terms of the patient, who must demonstrate the *desired end result*. The action taken to achieve the result may involve persons other than the patient; for example, if the patient is a child, the mother may be the learner[7, 8].

TABLE 2. PROBLEM LIST

FF NAME: Parsons

DATE	PROBLEM LIST	OBJECTIVES	RESULTS
	Parsons		
12/12/74	1. Lack of knowledge of urban resources	Family utilizes at least three urban resources by 6/25/75	6/25/75
12/12/74	2. Lack of knowledge regarding Kathy's heart condition	a) Family states five signs and symptoms of cardiac complications and necessary action to take and can describe basic physiology of circulatory system by 1/15/75.	
		b) Family allows child to perform all developmental tasks for age without overprotection for cardiac complications by 12/76.	1/15/75
12/12/74	3. Roaches in apartment	Roaches are reduced to a level acceptable to the family by 3/12/75.	3/12/75
12/12/74	4. Heart murmur	By 6/25/75, Kathy attends all scheduled BCC Cardiology Clinic appointments and follows all recommendations given by health personnel.	1/15/75 →

Each objective must provide information on five points: who, what, when, where, and how much. *Who* refers to the person/persons who must exhibit the desired behavior. *What* refers to the desired behavior. *When* is the time by which the end result should occur. *Where* refers to the place in which the desired result should occur. *How much* is the standard or the test by which the end result is evaluated[9].

The objectives must be measurable and, therefore, must contain an action verb, such as *demonstrate, state, list, increase, utilize*[10, 11]. All five points in the objective (*who, what, when, where, how much*) are criteria by which accomplishment of the objective is evaluated. These criteria must be realistic for the patient and specific to his problem. When answering these questions, the nurse uses established nursing standards, her own nursing knowledge and experience, and her own judgment and assessment of the family and/or patient. The problem list and objectives become a contract between the nurse and the family. They also become a table of contents for the entire family record[12].

The Parsons family was new to the city and had no relatives in the area; the only health or social resources they had used was the hospital for delivery. Because of this, one family problem identified was "Lack of knowledge of urban resources." Listed under the objective, *who*, is "the family"; listed under *what* is "utilizes urban resources"; *where* is understood to be in Richmond; *how much* is "at least three"; and *when* is "by June, 1975."

"At least three" was chosen because the public health nurse and family identified three resources that the family had already contacted, the Bureau of Crippled Children Clinic, Family Planning Clinic, and Pediatric Clinic. A time period of six months was chosen because the family members will have

had several return appointments to the clinics within this time. If the family keeps the appointments and follows recommendations, the public health nurse will be satisfied that the family will continue such activity. Thus, she will no longer have to deal with this problem.

For the second family problem, "Lack of knowledge regarding Kathy's heart murmur," the nurse formulated two objectives. Because of the urgency of the problem and the family's capability and eagerness to learn, the achievement period for the first objective was one month. By the end of the nurse's first visit, the family had some understanding of the condition. They had enough knowledge to take necessary action in response to evidence of complications. The achievement period for the second objective for this problem was longer—to allow the child to progress through several developmental tasks, especially those requiring much activity and independence.

The family's third problem, "Roaches in apartment" was identified by the family; roaches were not observed by the public health nurse. Therefore, the *how much* was written in terms of a reduced level acceptable to the family.

The objective for the fourth problem, which was Kathy's "Heart murmur," was formulated with her parents in mind, since they will be the learners. After Kathy's physical condition is completely diagnosed, this problem may need to be redefined and/or the objective written in terms of cure or maintenance. However, the nurse's initial objective is that Kathy is brought to all scheduled Cardiology Clinic appointments and that she and her parents follow all recommendations given by health personnel. From her own experience and her knowledge of the family, the nurse assumes that since these objectives were met, it is no longer a problem with which she has to deal.

Progress Notes

While the *objectives* are short-term and relate to specific problems of the patient/family, the *goals* are related to the long-term ultimate behavior of the patient/family. The goals are recorded on the family data base form and the patient data base form. Before the goals are written on the family record, a thorough assessment of the patient/family is needed. This requires several contacts between the nurse and the family[13].

On the progress notes, the public health nurse records the content of each contact with the patient/family. Also, she recorded contacts with other resources regarding the patient/family. Each recording contains the date and place of contact, the problem number and title dealt with, the name of the patient/family, and the nurse's signature.

Under each problem listed on the progress note, the nurse recorded the following elements:

Subjective data   (S)
Objective data   (O)
Action   (A)
Plan   (P)

According to the *Problem-Oriented Recording Orientation Manual*, the following definitions are given to the above:

Subjective data (S): Denotes the problem as the patient perceives it, his feelings, and variations he has noted. Subjective information, on the part of the nurse, her feelings and reactions, should also be recorded here. Any data not verifiable or observable by the nurse is subjective data.

Objective data (O): Includes physical and laboratory findings, observations, and developments related to the problem at hand. Avoid generalizations and hearsay. If a patient or a condition under discussion is not seen, then this should be noted.

Action (A): Action (including areas discussed) taken by the family, public health nurse, members of the health team, and any other person to alleviate the problem.

Plan (P): List of measures to be taken by family members, the nurse, or others in order to achieve mutually agreed upon objectives to solve the problem. The date of return visit is also recorded here[14].

Part of the planning and all of the implementation phase of nursing care for the Parsons family were recorded on the progress notes (Table 3). The methods for attaining the objectives were noted in the progress notes under P(*PLAN*). The implementation of the plans was noted under A(*ACTION*). These were not only the plans and actions of the public health nurse, but also of the family, patient, members of the health team, and any other person involved with the family care.

The *Problem-Oriented Recording Orientation Manual* does mention some exceptions to the guidelines for recording on the progress notes. If the subjective or objective data relating to a specific problem is recorded elsewhere in the family record, then the nurse can refer the reader to that location (e.g., "See Family Data Base"). If the nurse notes a passing episode that may or may not be identified as a problem for which the patient will need nursing assistance, she records in the problem list the pertinent data, as well as the action and plan under the heading Assessment* on the progress note[15]. For example, Frances had a urinary tract infection in the hospital. However, during the nurse's contact with her, Frances had no symptoms and was following physician's orders. The nurse concluded that she was coping with the situation and did not need nursing assistance at this time, but she

---

*The heading Assessment takes the place of a problem number and title.

TABLE 3. PROGRESS NOTES

FAMILY NAME: Parsons

DATE	Given Name	Significant health data; family plans; results obtained
12/12/74	PARSONS	HOME

1. LACK OF KNOWLEDGE OF URBAN RESOURCES
   - S: "We're new to the city and don't know where to take her (infant) if she gets sick," Frances stated.
   - O: Only community resource used: MCV Hospital for delivery.
   - A: PHN discussed reason and procedure for six-weeks checkup appointments at health department, BCC, MCV Pediatric Clinic.
   - P: Check to see that patient/family kept appointments.

2. LACK OF KNOWLEDGE REGARDING KATHY'S HEART CONDITION.
   - S: "I'm afraid she'll turn blue. I'm so afraid to leave her. We wanted a normal baby so badly," Frances stated.
   - O: Baby held by family during entire home visit.
   - A: PHN discussed heart murmur; signs and symptoms of cardiac complications, what to do if these occurred; baby's need for rest; and physiology of the circulatory system.
   - P: 1) Have parent recall signs and symptoms of cardiac complications and actions to take, and describe physiology of circulatory system 1/15/75.
     2) Observe if mother allows child to do developmental tasks for age without overconcern 1/15/75.
     3) Discuss growth and development in relation to child's age 1/15/75.
     4) Discuss cardiac catheterization on 1/15/75.
     5) Further explore the mother's statement, "wanted normal baby so badly."

noted in the plans that she would check the result of the urinalysis done at the six-weeks checkup clinic visit.

Another type of progress note in the family record of the Richmond City Health Department is the medical findings sheet, where the nurse records contacts between patient and physician. These medical find-ings and physician's orders are recorded in chronological sequence, with a separate medical findings sheet for each patient. They also are recorded under the problem number and title to which they relate[16]. This is where the nurse will record reports of Kathy's Cardiology Clinic visits for treatment of problem 4, "Heart Murmur."

The public health nurse visited the Parsons family four times between December, 1974, and June, 1975. The nursing plan, the nursing guidance and care given to the family, and the completion of stated objectives were recorded subsequent to each visit. The nurse based the evaluation of her nursing care on the achievement of the stated objectives. All five criteria (*who, what, when, where, how much*) had to be met before the objectives were considered to be achieved. When the criteria were met, the nurse entered the date in the results column of the problem list. In case of an ongoing or long-term objective, the nurse would enter the date in the problem sheet's results column over an arrow (1/15/75), indicating that some definitive action has been initiated to meet the objective[17].

During the public health nurse's home visit on January 13, 1975, Earl and Frances stated five signs and symptoms of cardiac complications and the necessary actions to take, and they described the basic physiology of the circulatory system. Therefore, the date 1/15/75 was put into the result column (see Table 2). During this visit the nurse learned that Kathy had attended her first Cardiology Clinic, and that the family was following recommendations. The date 1/15/75 over an arrow (1/15/75) was placed in the results column for problem 4, because definitive action to meet the objective had been initiated.

During the nurse's next home visit on March 12, 1975, roaches had been reduced to a level acceptable to the family. By June 25, 1975, Frances had made two visits to the Family Planning Clinic. Kathy had been to the Pediatric Clinic three times, had a cardiac catheterization, and had visited the Cardiology Clinic three times.

If the objectives had not been met, the nurse would have entered a date in the results column of the problem list, with the notation *unresolved*. The date would refer to a date on the progress note, which would give reasons why the objective was not met. From her reassessment (assuming the problem remained the same), the nurse would list the same problem number and title and would redefine the objective with the family. If the problem needed redefinition, then she and the family would formulate a new problem title and number and objective.

If an old problem was directly related to a new problem, then the nurse would draw an arrow with a date over it and write "Due to Number _____" (problem). The date over the arrow would refer to a date listed in the progress note, where the new problem is identified. The additional problem would be added to the problem list and an objective identified for it.

Thus, the public health nurse's evaluation of her nursing care is ongoing and is done mutually with the patient/family. When all the objectives have been met, the family is closed to nursing service. Of course, the nurse realizes that for some families all the objectives may not be met. After sufficient quantitative and qualitative nursing care has been given, a decision will have to be made. The contract with the family, the problem list and objectives, must be reviewed for possible extention, renegotiation, or termination of service.

Whatever the choice, the nurse can be satisfied that she has promoted quality nursing care for the family through use of problem-oriented recording. She can document all aspects of the nursing process—assessment, planning, implementation, and evaluation. The behavioral objectives allow her to compare expected outcomes with actual outcomes. This comparison lays the foundation for changing the plan and modifying practice, a most essential ingredient for assuring quality in nursing care throughout the patient's care.

REFERENCES

1. Aradine, C. R. and Guthneck, M. The problem-oriented record in a family health service. *Am. J. Nurs.*, Vol. 74, 1974, pp. 1108–1112.

2. Bloom, J. T., et al. Problem-oriented charting. *Am. J. Nurs.*, Vol. 71, 1971, pp. 2144–2148.

3. Woody, M. and Mallison, M. The problem-oriented system for patient-centered care. *Am. J. Nurs.*, Vol. 73, 1973, pp. 1169–1175.

4. *Problem-Oriented Recording Orientation Manual.* Bureau of Public Health Nursing, Richmond City Health Department, Richmond, Virginia, January, 1974, p. 14.

5. *POR Manual,* p. 14.

6. *POR Manual,* p. 16.

7. Mager, R. *Preparing Instructional Objectives.* Palo Alto, Cal.: Fearon, 1962, p. 2.

8. Smith, D. M. Writing objectives as a nursing practice skill. *Am. J. Nurs.,* Vol. 71, 1971, pp. 319–320.

9. *POR Manual,* 1974, p. 16.

10. Mager, 1962, p. 13–24.

11. Smith, 1971, p. 319–320.

12. *POR Manual,* 1974, p. 17.

13. *POR Manual,* p. 16.

14. *POR Manual,* p. 20.

15. *POR Manual,* p. 21.

16. *POR Manual,* p. 24.

17. *POR Manual,* p. 24.

Chapter 17

Nursing Standards Met and Unmet: A Community Client

Mary Beth Hanner
Marion E. Nicholls

Chronic illness is a major health problem of our time. Cardiac disease ranks high among the causes of chronic illness. Within the category of cardiac disease is a large population of clients whose cardiac problems impose moderate limitations on their activities. This case study relates to a client whose problem fits this classification.

Experience with clients in this group demonstrates that, while each client is unique and has individual nursing problems, many nursing problems are common to much of the group. Clients should be able to expect a certain minimum standard of nursing care to help them deal with these common problems. This case study is focused on three such common problems: (1) maintaining cardiac status, (2) increasing inadequate financial resources, and (3) maintaining independent status.

CASE STUDY

The client, Mrs. A., who is a sixty-year-old widow with no children was recently discharged from a hospital, where she was treated for a mycocardial infarction. Her only close relative is a sister who lives in California. They maintain contact through periodic letters, but they do not have a close relationship. Mrs. A. says that her landlady, Mrs. J., seems more like a sister to her. They have been friends ever since Mrs. A. moved into her present room after her husband died. The room she rents is a large bed-sitting room on the first floor of a three-story brownstone house, converted into light housekeeping units. Her room has an alcove containing a sink, a two-burner electric plate, and a small refrigerator. She shares a bathroom with the tenants who occupy the only other apartment on the first floor. The house is located in a formerly prosperous, middle-income neighborhood that is rapidly deteriorating. The community is economically depressed and at the time of this study had a 12 percent unemployment rate.

The landlady and her tenants have a "family relationship," and all were very supportive of Mrs. A. during her illness. Mrs. J. and Mrs. A. are especially good friends, spending a lot of time together shopping, playing bingo, and watching television. When Mrs. A.'s husband died ten years ago, she discovered that she was left with no income and no marketable skills except housekeeping. She is very independent, wanting no part of "charity," and she had been supporting herself by working as a cleaning lady for several families. She had saved some money, but her savings were not sufficient to support her without work. An insurance policy financed most of the hospital and medical bills from her recent hospitalization.

Upon discharge from the hospital, Mrs. A. was referred to the local community health agency for supervision of her diet, medications, and activities. Her referral form listed her diagnosis as: coronary insufficiency; mild myocardial infarction; congestive heart failure, class II (C). Her medical orders included: Digitoxin .125 mg q.d.; Diuril .5 gm q.o.d.; 1,200 calorie, 2 gm sodium-restricted diet; graduated program for resumption of activities; return to cardiology clinic in three weeks.

Mrs. A. received dietary counseling and exchange lists. The physician added a note that she could not return to her former employment. The referral form did not contain any extensive information on the client's knowledge of her condition and its management, and the information on her present cardiac status was limited. Therefore, comprehensive baseline data were not available to the nurse on her initial visit.

On the first home visit, the nurse found Mrs. A. to be a short, plump woman who stated that her height was 5 ft. 2 in., and her weight was 149 pounds. She was obviously concerned about her future, for she saw her savings melting away as she paid the balance of her hospital and medical bills. This left her with little to support herself while she recuperated, and she saw no source of income for the future since she could no longer work as a cleaning lady. She vowed that she would not be a "charity case." Although not all data could be collected on the first visit, enough was obtained to identify the following problems:

1. Congestive heart failure, class II (C)
2. Inadequate knowledge of cardiac problems and therapy:
   a. activity
   b. diet
   c. medication
3. Obesity
4. Inadequate financial resources
5. Threat to self-image (possible loss of independence)

Mrs. A. participated in the identification of her health care problems and in setting goals for her care. Both the client and nurse brought personal goals, values, and knowledge to this discussion. In any such exchange, the nurse brings authoritative knowledge and experience, plus an awareness of the resources available to achieve the goals. By combining client goals with authoritative nursing standards and knowledge of available resources, the nurse-client team should be able to produce achievable goals.

The client and nurse agreed that Mrs. A. would attain her optimal level of functioning through achievement of the following long-range goals:

Goal 1. Modification of her lifestyle to adapt to the limitations imposed by her cardiac status.

Goal 2. Maintenance of her self-image as an independent, productive member of the community.

In order to achieve long-range goals, many short-term objectives need to be set. These objectives then become standards against which progress toward goal achievement can be measured. In Table 1, selected objectives are identified and some nursing interventions are described. The objectives are described as ends standards and nursing interventions as means standards. The list of items is representative rather than exhaustive. The objectives and plans cited are the initial ones; outcomes describe the client's status at the end of six months.

As indicated in Table 1, objectives 1 and 2 were met and contributed to the achievement of the broader goal of modification of her lifestyle to adapt to the limitations imposed by her cardiac status. The nursing interventions (means standards) describe activities that any nurse caring for Mrs. A. or any client with similar problems might be expected to plan and implement.

Means standard 1A deals with monitoring the client's cardiac status. In order to ensure consistency in monitoring from nurse to nurse and/or client to client, parameters should be established. These parameters could be expressed in the form of a guide or a cardiac monitoring flow sheet. Either tool would direct the nurse to meet at least a minimum standard for monitoring. Use of such standards would increase consistency of care without interfering with individualization. If such minimum standards do not exist, each nurse must design a monitoring system for each client and the quality of such monitoring systems depends upon the competency of the practitioner designing them. Without generally accepted minimum standards, clients having similar problems could receive a wide range of quality of care.

Objective 2, also derived from long-range goal 1, is another standard applicable to a wide group of clients. In order to provide all such clients with knowledge to enable them to identify signs and symptoms and take appropriate action, nurses need to develop a basic teaching plan. Such teaching plans could include a check list on which the progress of the client could be indicated. Again, the plan could be individualized, while at the same time there could be increased assurance that every client received the knowledge needed to meet the objective.

Objective 3, relating to financial assistance, was met through the provision of public assistance funds. This contributed to the achievement of the broad goal, modification of Mrs. A.'s lifestyle. However, the need to accept Social Security Income and Medicaid increased Mrs. A.'s feelings of dependence and helplessness and lowered her self-esteem. Thus, long-range goal 2 was actually hampered by the achievement of objective 3.

The joint efforts of the nurse and social worker contributed to the achievement of objective 3. The increasing focus on the interdisciplinary team approach to client care is another factor that affects the setting of nursing standards. The team providing care to clients includes not only nurses but also social workers, physical therapists, speech therapists, and many others. Often, the team in a community agency sets joint goals for client care, and several or all team members may be involved in the implementation of the plan.

Although each member of the team has some specific functions, many functions overlap and may be carried out by several members of the team. For example, the nurse's role in obtaining financial assistance for clients may vary according to the availability of social workers in the agency. The community health nurse may need to act as a coordinator and liaison between the client and the social worker. In this case the nurse initially suggested potential sources of financial assistance to the client; she participated in a conference with Mrs. A. and the social worker; and she helped the client complete the necessary forms to apply

TABLE 1.

Objectives for six-month Period (Ends Standard)	Nursing Plan (Means Standard)	Actual Outcomes at Six Months

1. Cardiac status will remain stable or improve as evidenced by selected signs such as pulse, b.p., weight, edema, etc. Unfavorable changes will be noted and appropriate action taken.	1. A. Establish baseline cardiac status.
	   1. Take baseline cardiac history.
	   2. Do cardiac physical assessment to establish status on first visit.
	   3. Validate findings with Mrs. A's physician.
	B. Monitor Mrs. A's status on each visit and record findings on cardiac flow sheet.
		1. A. Data base was collected and is on file in the record. Physician validated findings via telephone consultation.
		
		B. Cardiac status was monitored q. week/1 mo.; q. 2–3 wks/2 mos.; q. 1 mo./3 mos. by nurse. (Examples of evidence of cardiac status monitored: pulse rate stable at 60–70/min. at rest; client able to climb one flight of stairs without shortness of breath, walk an increased number of city blocks without fatigue; no episodes of angina after 3 mos.)

	C. Respond to changes in status.
	   1. Provide counseling on needed changes in health behavior.
	   2. Refer to clinic or emergency room.
		C. Mrs. A. called nurse at end of 2nd week and reported shortness of breath and an episode of angina following overexertion. After assessment by the nurse, she was advised to increase her rest periods.

2. Can verbalize signs and symptoms of changes in cardiac status and describe action to be taken.	2. Teach Mrs. A. to identify signs and symptoms of change in cardiac status and to take appropriate actions to counteract the change. (For example: reduce activities, check diet for indiscretions.) A specific teaching plan will be formulated.	2. In all instances, she verbalized actions she would take that were appropriate. (For example: adjustment of activity as a result of occurrence of angina, stricter adherence to low sodium diet after noticeable edema.)

Objectives for six-month Period (Ends Standard)	Nursing Plan (Means Standard)	Actual Outcomes at Six Months
3. Mrs. A. will obtain adequate financial assistance to meet her needs. (A minimum of $200.00 per month.)	3. A. Arrange a joint conference with the agency social worker, the nurse and Mrs. A. Explore Mrs. A's eligibility for Social Security Assistance, Supplemental Security Income, Medicaid, Food Stamps, etc. B. Coordinate all efforts to obtain financial assistance. Arrange transportation to Social Services offices, if needed.	3. At first, Mrs. A. refused to meet with the social worker, but as her savings diminished, she agreed to the conference. She qualified for Supplemental Security Income and Medicaid, which gave her a monthly income of $218.50. Medicaid covered many of her medical expenses. Although she said the nurse and the social worker were "as nice as they could be," she still felt like a charity case," and would accept the assistance as a temporary measure only until she could go back to work.
4. Mrs. A. will obtain full or part-time sedentary employment.	4. During joint conferences with the social workers, explore potential sources for employment.	4. The social worker found some work that involved stuffing envelopes at home. The pay was meager, and Mrs. A. would not accept the job. No other suitable employment was found.

for funds. The nurse and the social worker performed both separate and overlapping activities.

Although financial problems are frequently encountered by those with a chronic illness, the need for assistance does not apply to the entire group. Although objective 3 would not be set for all clients in the population, the financial resources of all clients should be assessed to determine if they are adequate.

Objective 4 was a direct outcome of Mrs. A.'s desperate need to maintain her independence. While there are a number of ways an individual can achieve this, to Mrs. A., independence meant full-time employment. For this reason, the nurse and Mrs. A. agreed that suitable employment was a desirable nursing goal. However, at the end of six months, the objective was not met, and there seemed little likelihood that it would be met.

This failure raises the question of whether this was a realistic goal in view of Mrs. A.'s age, physical limitations, lack of marketable skills, and her location in an economically depressed area. The possibilities for her full-time employment were slight. Furthermore, the appropriateness of this objective as a nursing goal is questionable. This was an operational objective designed to contribute to attainment of the long-range goal of maintaining the client's self-image as a contributing member of the community. The long-range goal was an appropriate nursing goal, but the operational objective to find employment for her was not. Nurses are seldom qualified as employment counselors, nor do they have immediate access to sources for employment. This objective is a social service objective rather than a nursing objective and, as such, it should not appear on a nursing care plan. However, it may be an interdisciplinary goal requiring that various members of the team contribute to its achievement. The social worker could locate employment that met the requirements for activity set by the doctor; the nurse might monitor the impact of the job on the client.

Since it is obvious that Mrs. A. feels threatened by a loss of control over her environment, a more appropriate nursing objective would have been: Mrs. A. will maintain her self-esteem as evidenced by verbal expressions of a positive self-image and increasing involvement in productive social activities (e.g., volunteer work, learning new skills, etc.). Nursing intervention could then focus on counseling, orientation to resources, and encouragement of participation in appropriate activities.

SUMMARY

There are populations of clients having similar nursing care problems. Minimum nursing standards for these groups can be identified. Such minimum nursing standards would not have to interfere with individualization of care, but would help to ensure consistency in the quality of care.

Evaluation of the outcomes in this case study demonstrates that achievement of certain standards can be attributed to nursing inervention, while the achievement of other standards is not so directly related to nursing care. As interdisciplinary teams in community health agencies become more common, the problem of identifying outcomes resulting directly from nursing care increases. Thus, it may be necessary to use process as well as outcome standards in evaluating the quality of nursing care.

INDEX

INDEX